Graffiti in the Southwest Conference

Other Books In This Series:

GRAFFITI
IN THE
SOUTHWEST
CONFERENCE

**Marina N. Haan
Richard B. Hammerstrom**

WARNER BOOKS

A Warner Communications Company

Warner Books, Inc.,
75 Rockefeller Plaza,
New York, N. Y. 10019

W A Warner Communications Company

Cover design by Gene Light

Cover art by Jack Davis

Artistic enhancement by Jerry Mymudes,
Marina Haan, and Richard Hammerstrom

First printing: September 1981

10 9 8 7 6 5 4 3 2 1

Printed in the United States of America

Library of Congress Cataloging in Publication Data

Haan, Marina N.
    Graffiti in the Southwest Conference.

    1. Graffiti—Texas.   2. Graffiti—Oklahoma.
3. Graffiti—Arkansas.   4. Students—Texas—Atti-
tudes.   5. Students—Oklahoma—Attitudes.
6. Students—Arkansas—Attitudes.   7. Southwest
Conference (U.S.)   I. Hammerstrom, Richard B.
II. Title.
GT3913.T4H3   081   81–3360
ISBN 0–446–37004–5 (U.S.A.) AACR2
ISBN 0–446–37084–3 (Canada)

DEDICATION

This book is dedicated to the technicians of toilet-stall design for providing new and more creative challenges to the graffitiist's technologies.

AUTHORS' NOTE

"Current census reports show a dramatic shift in U.S. population from the Northeast to the Southwest."

Wire Service Report

Why does God send all you Yankees down here to bother us Texans?

Texas Tech–Holden Hall

Why, indeed? Why is a major portion of the population of the Northeast packing its belongings and heading to the Southwest?

Some say it's the weather. Others say jobs. Still others say they go because the people are friendlier in the Southwest. But there is another group going to the Southwest: the students heading to the universities of the Southwest Conference.

It was with this latter group, the students, that we were most interested. We wondered why they chose the Southwest over other schools. We also wondered what they would find when they arrived on campus in the Southwest Conference.

We decided that we would find out about these students. We packed our own bags and set out to investigate the schools in the Southwest Conference.

Having been warned about a tendency among people in the Southwest to exaggerate a bit, we decided not to gather our information through conversations. Rather, we determined that we should go to the one source of information that is provided freely and openly, the one source available to all, the one source that does not distinguish between native and newcomer. We decided to learn about the Southwest Conference through the graffiti written on the desks and walls of its various campuses.

We have consolidated our findings and have presented them on the following pages. We feel that this information provides a vivid description of life in the Southwest Conference and goes a long way toward explaining the reason for the migration to the Southwest.

Marina N. Haan
Richard B. Hammerstrom

CONTENTS

Graffiti in the Southwest Conference

If God had meant
for Texans to ski

He would have made
bullshit white!

ARKANSAS – WATERMAN HALL

One immediately notices the regional pride displayed in the Southwest Conference.

Question: How do you know you're in West Texas?
Answer: Go west til you smell it and south til you step in it.

Dallas – Fort Worth Airport

I'VE ONLY BEEN IN TEXAS ONE WEEK AND ALREADY KNOW THAT BOOTS WEREN'T JUST MADE FOR WALKIN'.

HOUSTON – FLEMING BUILDING

Anywhere in Texas is where it's at.

U of Texas – Welch Hall

1

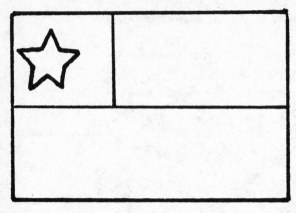

SECEDE!

SOUTHERN METHODIST (SMU) –
FONDREN SCIENCE BUILDING

GOD CREATED TEXAS ON THE 8TH DAY.

TEXAS CHRISTIAN – RICHARDSON
BUILDING

There would be no Texas if the Alamo had a back door.

Dallas – Fort Worth Airport

IF IGNORANCE WAS PLUTONIUM, THE MOST
ERUDITE TEXAN COULD BLOW UP THE WORLD.

U OF TEXAS –
BUSINESS/ECONOMICS

Question: How do you spot a Texas driver?
Answer: He's the one swerving to hit pedestrians.

– below –

Question: How do you tell if a Texas driver goes to Church?
Answer: Only if he goes to Church will he go up on the sidewalk to get 'em.

– below –

Question: How do you tell a "true Christian" from a Texas driver.
Answer: The "true Christians" don't back up for a second try.

Rice – Keith Weiss Geology Labs

QUESTION: WHAT IS A TEXAS VIRGIN?
ANSWER: A GIRL WHO CAN RUN FASTER THAN HER BROTHER.

DALLAS – FORT WORTH AIRPORT

QUESTION: WHAT IS AN ARKANSAS VIRGIN?
ANSWER: AN UGLY 5TH GRADER.

ARKANSAS – CHEMISTRY
BUILDING

Not all Texans suck, only those that stay in Texas.

Arkansas – Communications Building

4

Occasional reference is made to those of us not favored with a Texas/Arkansas origin. Don't worry, it is all in jest . . . isn't it?

YANKEES ARE FLATLAND SNOW LILIES.
U OF TEXAS – GEOLOGY

Here I sit, about to uncork 'er,
giving birth to another New Yorker.
Texas Tech – Holden Hall

BEING FROM NEW YORK IS NEVER HAVING TO SAY YOU'RE SORRY.

– BELOW –

BECAUSE IT'S OBVIOUS.

– BELOW –

BECAUSE DOING SO WHENEVER IT WAS APPROPRIATE WOULD BE A LIFE'S WORK.
U OF TEXAS – LAW

SEND ME BACK TO NEW YORK CITY.
RICE – SEWELL HALL

There is a school in the East called M.I.T. What does M-I-T stand for?

— below —

Mycanean Ink Traders

— below —

Misplaced Intellectual Turkeys

— below —

Marthas Intestinal Tract

— below —

My It's Terrible

— below —

Made in Turkey, Taiwan, Tunisia, etc.

— below —

Massachusetts Imported Tectonicians

— below —

My Itching Tube

— below —

Make It Twitch

— below —

Many Idiodic Things

Rice – Keith Weiss Geological Labs

MASSAH CHEWS SHITS!

RICE – KEITH WEISS
GEOLOGICAL LABS

The West is the best!

Texas A&M – Scoates Hall

CALIFORNIANS ARE LIKE A BOWL OF CEREAL—NUTS, FRUITS AND FLAKES.

U OF TEXAS – WELCH HALL

U of Houston is a baby-sitting service.

HOUSTON – LIBRARY

Southwest students are quick to inform newcomers of the special attributes of their respective campuses.

God help this school!

Houston – Heyne Building

I THINK HEYNE BUILDING SUCKS! IT'S LIKE A DUNGEON DOWN HERE.

– BELOW –

"H" BUILDING IS NOT HEYNE BUILDING. IT REFERS TO "HELL-HOLE" BUILDING.

HOUSTON – HEYNE BUILDING

Houston Cougars are pussies!

Arkansas – Psychology

HAVE YOU HEARD THE LATEST AGGIE JOKE?
FOOTBALL!

TEXAS A&M – TEAGUE
RESEARCH CENTER

QUESTION: WHAT DO YOU CALL A GOOD-LOOKING GIRL AT TEXAS A&M?
ANSWER: VISITING.

U OF TEXAS – GEOLOGY

Question: Why don't Aggie women use vibrators?
Answer: They chip their teeth.

Houston – Law

AGGIES MAKE BETTER LOVERS.

– BELOW –

DREAM ON!

– BELOW –

WHY DO YOU THINK ALL THOSE PIGS ARE SMILING DOWN AT THE PIG BARN?

TEXAS A&M – CONFERENCE
CENTER

Aggies do it unto udders.

Rice – Sewell Hall

NO WHERE ELSE BUT AGGIEVILLE!

*TEXAS A&M – CONFERENCE
CENTER*

GIG 'EM AGGIES!

*TEXAS A&M – CONFERENCE
CENTER*

I hate this university!

– below –

Highway 6 goes both ways.

Texas A&M – Evans Library

NUKE THE WAGGIES!

TEXAS A&M – SCOATES HALL

**Thank God for the Corps, it keeps the ugly girls off the
street and out of our hair.**

Texas A&M – Heldenfels Hall

*IF IT WEREN'T FOR THE CORPS, THERE NEVER WOULD
HAVE BEEN AN A&M.*

– BELOW –

IF IT WEREN'T FOR A&M, THERE NEVER WOULD HAVE BEEN A CORPS.

– BELOW –

. . . OR CROPS, FOR THAT MATTER, TO SPELL IT ANOTHER WAY.

> *TEXAS A&M – HELDENFELS HALL*

JOIN THE CORPS, LEARN TO KILL.

> ***TEXAS A&M – HELDENFELS HALL***

The few.
The proud.
The non-regs.

> *Texas A&M – Francis Hall*

(ARROW POINTING TO TOILET PAPER)
AGGIE BIRTH CERTIFICATES.

> *HOUSTON – FLEMING BUILDING*

(arrow pointing to toilet paper)
Aggie Gift Certificates.

> ***SMU – Fincher Building***

MAKE THIS PLACE ANOTHER A&M—JOIN THE ROTC.

> *RICE – RAYZOR HALL*

THE QUESTION OF LIFE—IS IT TRUE THAT OWLS ARE JUST REFORMED AGGIES?

RICE – ANDERSON BIO LABS

How come they're smarter at Rice?

– below –

They give a hoot.

Texas Tech – Holden Hall

QUESTION: WHAT'S THE DIFFERENCE BETWEEN RICE WOMEN AND GARBAGE?
ANSWER: GARBAGE GETS TAKEN OUT AT LEAST ONCE A WEEK.

RICE – MECHANICAL LABS

Rice women are the most beutiful and the most fun.

– below –

But they can't spell for shit.

– below –

But they can spell for sex.

Rice – Library

TCU IS FULL OF STUCK-UP SORORITY BITCHES.

*TEXAS CHRISTIAN – SADLER
ADMINISTRATION*

12

TCU IS ONE HELL OF A PLACE TO WORK.

TEXAS CHRISTIAN – SCOTT HALL

Nuke TCU!

Texas Christian – Richardson Building

TCU ... COTTON BOWL IN 1984 ... YOU CAN COUNT ON IT.

TEXAS CHRISTIAN – SADLER
ADMINISTRATION

SMU will be beaten by Baylor, Texas, Houston, Arkansas, Tech and A&M.

SMU – Fincher Building

SMU SUCKS!

TEXAS CHRISTIAN –
RICHARDSON BUILDING

TECH FOOTBALL SUCKS!

TEXAS TECH – LIBRARY

Beat Texas!

Texas Tech – Library

TECH BITES WEENIES!

TEXAS TECH – HOLDEN HALL

Lubbock girls only do in a pinch—or in a squeeze.

Texas Tech – Fat Dawg's

I HATE LUBBOCK!

– BELOW –

AND LUBBOCK HATES YOU. TOWNS ARE FUNNY THAT WAY.

TEXAS TECH – ART

U OF TEXAS—IF GOD WAS GONNA GIVE THE WORLD AN ENEMA, THIS IS WHERE HE WOULD STICK IT IN.

U OF TEXAS – MOORE HALL

TU sucks!

Texas A&M – Conference Center

TEA SIPS SUCK!

TEXAS A&M – CONFERENCE CENTER

This place reeks of oil.

U of Texas – Sutton Hall

UT MONEY + OIL + TREES + CEMENT = EXOCRETIC REACTION.

U OF TEXAS – TOWNES LAW

14

LONGHORNS #100!

TEXAS TECH – LIBRARY

Longhorns #1!

– below –

Their I.Q.

– below –

Their sperm count.

Texas Christian – Dan Rogers Hall

HOOK 'EM HORNS!

TEXAS A&M – HELDENFELS HALL

Kilroy says, "Hook 'em horns!"

SMU – Florence Hall

HOOK 'EM HORNS!
LONGHORN MANIA!
NO PLACE LIKE TEXAS!

SMU – FLORENCE HALL

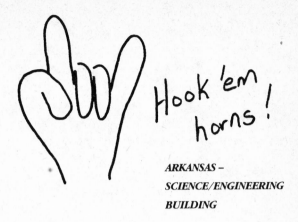

Hook 'em horns!

ARKANSAS – SCIENCE/ENGINEERING BUILDING

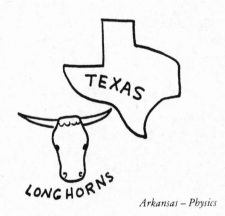

Arkansas – Physics

U OF TEXAS STUDENTS ARE LIKE FARTS:

THEY ARE LOUD.

THEY STINK.

THEY NEVER GO BACK TO WHERE THEY COME FROM.

WE NEVER WANTED THEM IN THE FIRST PLACE.

THEY GENERALLY RISE ABOVE THEIR POINT OF ORIGIN.

HOUSTON – ENGINEERING BUILDING

Did you hear about the T-sip who tried to blow up a school bus? Burned his lips on the exhaust pipe.

Texas A&M – Dogherty Building

U OF TEXAS STUDENTS ARE LIKE JELLY. THAT'S FROM TOO MUCH DOPE AND TOO LITTLE UPSTAIRS.

HOUSTON – ENGINEERING
BUILDING

DO YOU KNOW WHY THEY NEVER HAVE CHRISTMAS AT TEXAS UNIVERSITY? BECAUSE THEY DON'T HAVE THREE WISE MEN OR A VIRGIN.

– BELOW –

DOES THAT MEAN WE CAN'T HAVE EASTER BECAUSE WE DON'T HAVE ANY BUNNIES?

BAYLOR – RICHARDSON SCIENCE

Geologists take their rocks out and play with them.

Texas Christian – Richardson Building

There are always good reasons for pursuing a particular field of study offered at the schools of the Southwest Conference.

GEOLOGY IS A GUESSING GAME.

ARKANSAS – ENGINEERING BUILDING

Geologists are really down to earth.

U of Texas – Geology

I DROPPED GEOLOGY BECAUSE I DIDN'T WANT TO CHANGE DIAPERS ALL MY LIFE.

RICE – GEOLOGY

NEW WAVE GEOLOGY! PUNK ROCK!

U OF TEXAS – GEOLOGY

Geologist's breakfast—rock 'n roll.

U of Texas – Geology

GEOLOGISTS DIG COUNTRY ROCK.
BUT IT AIN'T ALWAYS GNEISS.

RICE – GEOLOGY

Astronomers have vast spaces in their minds.

U of Texas – Moore Hall

PHYSICS SUCKS ALMOST AS BAD AS FRATS.

U OF TEXAS – PAINTER HALL

FYSICS IS PHUCKED!

U OF TEXAS – MOORE HALL

Let's go to war; I'm bored with Chemistry.

Arkansas – Business Administration

BIOLOGY GROWS ON YOU.

HOUSTON – SCIENCE BUILDING

Biologists get small.

U of Texas – Painter Hall

BIO CHEM IS A PUSSY.

HOUSTON – FLEMING BUILDING

BIO CHEMISTRY IS A BIOLOGICAL MYSTERY.

U OF TEXAS – WELCH HALL

Have you ever met a pre-Med that didn't have a brown nose?

Texas A&M – Herman Heep Building

PRE-MEDS: AMERICA'S INVESTMENT IN
OBNOXIOUSNESS.

U OF TEXAS – WELCH HALL

**Theology: everything you always wanted to know about
nothing but were afraid to ask.**

– below –

I wouldn't know God if I ran into hymn.

Rice – Library

TAKE LATIN, YOU'LL LOVE IT.

RICE – RAYZOR HALL

TRIVIA FREAKS DO WELL IN HISTORY COURSES.

*TEXAS A&M – TEAGUE RESEARCH
CENTER*

Econ gives head!

Rice – Sewell Hall

ACCOUNTING IS FUN.

TEXAS CHRISTIAN – DAN ROGERS HALL

Math majors are fuckin' weird.

– below –

Ah, but at least we're fucking.

Texas Christian – Winton Scott Building

STATISTICS IS LIKE A BIKINI—WHAT SHOWS IS REAL, BUT WHAT IS HIDDEN IS VITAL.

TEXAS A&M – TEAGUE RESEARCH CENTER

GREAT FUTURE IN CONSULTING.

U OF TEXAS – GRADUATE SCHOOL OF BUSINESS

428 was created so that seniors could flunk one more class before completing the sentence given them.

Texas A&M – Dogherty Building

PARADOX = 2 PhD's
PARADISE = 1 PhD + 1 JOB

U OF TEXAS – PAINTER HALL

Ever fuck a sheep?

– below –

No, but I fucked a grad student once. Isn't that the same?
Rice – Mechanical Lab

YOU SHOULD CONSIDER GLASS-BLOWING.
BAYLOR – MARRS MCLEAN
SCIENCE

RADIO AND T.V. IS SUCH A CUTE MAJOR.

– BELOW –

DON'T GIVE US ANY STATIC.
BAYLOR – MARRS MCLEAN
SCIENCE

Drama is for people who can't face accounting.
U of Texas – Winship Drama Building

MUSIC MAJORS DO IT WITH FOUR BEATS TO THEIR MEASURE.
HOUSTON – FINE ARTS

Art majors are plastic fools who conform to nonconformity.

Houston – Art & Architecture
Annex

ART—SOMETHING ONE HAS A TALENT FOR.
U OF TEXAS – GEOLOGY

IF WHAT THE PEOPLE IN THIS BUILDING PRODUCE IS ART, THEN GARBAGE MAN IS JUST ANOTHER PHRASE FOR ART COLLECTOR.

HOUSTON – ART &
ARCHITECTURE ANNEX

For every ten art majors, there is one artist.

Houston – Art & Architecture Annex

ARCHITECTURE!

ARKANSAS – MEMORIAL HALL

God bless architecture and all it stands for.

Arkansas – Vol Walker Hall

ARCHITECTS DREAM. ENGINEERS KNOW.
U OF TEXAS – GOLDSMITH HALL

WHAT WOULD YOU COMPARE WITH ARCHITECTURE? HEMORRHOIDS.

ARKANSAS – VOL WALKER HALL

Architecture: the final frontier.

Texas Tech – Library

WHAT IS THE OUTSTANDING QUALITY OF ARCHITECTURE? SUPERFICIALITY.

ARKANSAS – VOL WALKER HALL

Architectural engineers have better erections.

U of Texas – Goldsmith Hall

NINETY PERCENT OF ARCHITECTURE COULD BE TAUGHT IN BUSINESS ADMINISTRATION.

ARKANSAS – VOL WALKER HALL

ARCHITECTS MAKE BETTER LOVERS.

– BELOW –

YEH, ANYBODY IS MADE BETTER NEXT TO THEM.

U OF TEXAS – GOLDSMITH HALL

I just want to change the way things are with my work. So should you.

– below –

From time to time I sell my work, but it is not secure. I want to work with an engineer. Any engineering graduate type of work.

U of Texas – Art Building

ENGINEERS HAVE BIG TOOLS.

ARKANSAS – BUSINESS
ADMINISTRATION

Double your dipoles.
Double your flux.
Double E, Double E,
Double E sucks.

Houston – Engineering Building

AN ENGINEER TOLD ME BEFORE HE DIED, AND I HAVE NO REASON TO BELIEVE HE LIED.

RICE – KEITH WEISS
GEOLOGICAL LABS

HAS ANYONE EVER DIED FROM ENGINEERING MATH 151?

TEXAS A&M – DOGHERTY
BUILDING

Business and education aren't anything compared to engineering! You ought to try that if you want to complain about something.

U of Texas – Graduate School of
Business

B.Q.'S ARE THE LOWEST FORM OF LIFE ON EARTH.

TEXAS A&M – PHYSICS
BUILDING

Wanted: Two petroleum engineering professors for employment as mudflaps on my truck.

Texas A&M – Dogherty Building

FUCK ENGINEERING!

– BELOW –

DISRESPECTFUL!

– BELOW –

I MEANT NO DISRESPECT.

– BELOW –

THE BOY MEANT NO DISRESPECT.

– BELOW –

STILL, IT WAS DISRESPECTFUL, AND HE MUST BE PUNISHED.

– BELOW –

WELL, THEN, FUCK ENGINEERING!

U OF TEXAS – ENGINEERING
SCIENCE

PSYCHOLOGY—THE STUDY OF THE ID BY THE ODD.

U OF TEXAS – TOWNES LAW

Mine eyes have seen the glory
of the theories of Freud.
He taught me all the evils
that my ego must avoid.
Repression of the impulses
result in paranoid,
as the Id goes marching on.

Rice – Space Science

ARE WE NOT MEN? NO, WE ARE LAW SCHOOL
ANDROIDS.

U OF TEXAS – TOWNES LAW

Law School is bullshit!

Texas Tech – Law

*LAW SCHOOL REMINDS ME OF FISHING FOR CRABS: YOU
WAIT UNTIL THEY CRAWL INTO YOUR CAGE AND THEN
YOU PULL THEM UP AND BOIL THEM ALIVE.*

U OF TEXAS – TOWNES LAW

**LAW SCHOOL IS LIKE A WHOREHOUSE—PEOPLE PAY
GOOD MONEY AND GET SCREWED.**

– BELOW –

AND THEY DON'T EVEN GET A KISS.

ARKANSAS – WATERMAN HALL

What if Eve had offered to eat the apple? Contract?

– below –

Pactum nudum.

– below –

No, we would all be unclothed counsel in the Garden of Eden.

U of Texas – Townes Law

PRE-TRIAL MOTIONS ARE NOTHING MORE THAN JUDICIAL FOREPLAY.

U OF TEXAS – TOWNES LAW

If you law students would pay attention instead of playing with yourselves . . .

SMU – Storey Hall

IS A CONTRACT VOID AT INSEMINATION?

– BELOW –

NO, IT JUST MEANS SOMEONE GOT SCREWED.

U OF TEXAS – TOWNES LAW

WHAT'S A SMALL TORT? A TORTILLA.

U OF TEXAS – TOWNES LAW

If these clowns are in Law School, then who in Hell is running the circus?

Arkansas – Waterman Hall

TWO LAWYERS CAN LIVE IN A TOWN WHERE ONE CAN'T.

U OF TEXAS – TOWNES LAW

A lot of people who came here wanting to be lawyers stayed just to prove that they can make it.

Arkansas – Waterman Hall

WHY NO GRAFFITI IN THIS RESTROOM?

– BELOW –

LAW SCHOOL TEACHES YOU NOT TO STICK YOUR NECK OUT.

U OF TEXAS – TOWNES LAW

IF THAT SONOVABITCH, PENNOYER,
HAD ONLY PAID HIS LAWYER,
CIVIL PRO WOULD NOT FILL ME WITH SUCH DREAD.
MY EYES ARE RED AND BLEARY
FROM CONTEMPLATING <u>ERIE</u>
AND I WISH THAT TRAIN HAD LEFT OLD TOMPKINS
DEAD.
I CAN'T WAIT TO STUDY PLEADINGS,
PLENARY PROCEEDINGS,
AND THE THOUGHT OF INTERPLEADER LEAVES ME HIGH.
I'M INTO LEGAL FICTION,
BUT I'LL PASS ON JURISDICTION.
IF I HEAR THAT WORD ONCE MORE I THINK I'LL DIE.

– below –

AND WHAT WOULD BRANDEIS HAVE TO SAY ABOUT ALL
THIS? EXACTLY.

U OF TEXAS – TOWNES LAW

What the law has done to me is illegal!

Arkansas – Waterman Hall

I suffer from being exposed to school.

U OF TEXAS – PAINTER HALL

Students in the Southwest Conference experience many new developments in their personalities.

I think college creates crazy people.

– below –

I think crazies create college people.

Arkansas – Memorial Hall

AS I SIT HERE ACTING PRUDENT
I'M GIVING BIRTH TO ANOTHER STUDENT.

ARKANSAS – WATERMAN HALL

LATE NIGHTS AND EARLY MORNINGS—COLLEGE IS KILLING ME.

BAYLOR – RICHARDSON SCIENCE

FRUSTRATION

U of Texas – Undergrad Library

HAVE YOU SEEN BETTER DAYS?

U OF TEXAS – MOORE HALL

Beware of the creatures that lurk in the bowels of our building.

Texas A&M – Oceanography & Meteorology

NINE MILE SKID ON A TEN-MILE SLIDE, HOT AS A PISTOL BUT COOL INSIDE.

HOUSTON – ART & ARCHITECTURE

ARE WE NOT BEEF? NO, WE ARE BEVO!

U OF TEXAS – TOWNES LAW

I can resist anything but temptation.

U of Texas – Woolrich Hall

PEOPLE PUT US DOWN JUST BECAUSE WE GET AROUND.

RICE – MEMORIAL CENTER

Anyone who wants a friend, sign here. There just aren't too too many of those around anymore.

Rice – Library

ABOLISH HOSTILITY—KISS MY FRIENDLY ASS.

RICE – RAYZOR HALL

DON'T LET TENSION, ANGER OR HANDICAPS GET YOU DOWN—AFTER ALL, YOU'RE ONLY HUMAN.

U OF TEXAS – TOWNES LAW

Ha! Me worry?

U of Texas – Moore Hall

THOUGH I WALK THROUGH THE VALLEY OF DEATH, I FEAR NO EVIL, FOR I AM THE BADDEST SONOVABITCH IN THE VALLEY.

TEXAS TECH – HOLDEN HALL

I'm mad as Hell, and I'm not gonna take it any more.

U of Texas – Geology

MELLOW OUT OR YOU WILL PAY.

– BELOW –

GET DOWN OR BLOW UP.
> *U OF TEXAS – UNDERGRADUATE*
> *LIBRARY*

I'M SLACKING UP.
> ***RICE – MEMORIAL CENTER***

Transfer now, avoid the May rush.
> *Arkansas – Engineering Building*

SPRING STRIKE TENTATIVELY SCHEDULED FOR APRIL.

– BELOW –

SPRING TENTATIVELY SCHEDULED FOR MARCH.
> *U OF TEXAS – TOWNES LAW*

Football is to higher education what bullfighting is to agriculture.
> ***Rice – Rayzor Hall***

ANY TIME NOW AND I'LL ARRIVE.
> *U OF TEXAS – UNDERGRADUATE*
> *LIBRARY*

LET IT NOT BE SAID THAT I WAS NOWHERE.

TEXAS A&M – CIVIL
ENGINEERING BUILDING

Think of times when you're alone.
Think of times when you're home.
But don't think you're gonna get
out of here without paying.

Baylor – Marrs McLean Science

TO ALL FIRST YEARS—GIVE IT UP!

TEXAS TECH – LAW

All we have to fear is two more years of this.

Texas Tech – Law

*EDDIE C.—A MAN OF WEALTH, WIT AND A CERTAIN
LACK OF INTELLIGENCE.*

U OF TEXAS – UNDERGRADUATE
LIBRARY

IS THERE INTELLIGENT LIFE ON EARTH?

– below –

YES, BUT I'M ONLY VISITING.

U OF TEXAS – MOORE HALL

Intellectualism is a waste of time.

Texas Tech – Law

WE ARE ALL A LOST GENERATION.—CIRCA 1971

HOUSTON – FLEMING HALL

My mind is a surfboard.

U of Texas – Art

'SEE-THROUGH' LIVES.

U OF TEXAS – BATTLE HALL

STUPID PUPPETS.

U OF TEXAS – GRADUATE
SCHOOL OF BUSINESS

Indeed, the gods were bored, so they created Adam. He was bored, so Eve was created. Thus, they were bored together . . . boring . . . bores . . . bored . . . until we arrive at me, so bored that I will make the effort to recount the story of primal boredom while writing at this impossible angle. My wrist hurts and I am still bored and boring.

– below –

Before I became a teenage nihilist I was a fetal nihilist. My first words were 'womb/room/tomb'. When I read Tolkien and met the trees who had become immobile, I became an Entistentialist . . . ha . . . ha . . . ha . . . I'm bored and boring . . . still.

Arkansas – Communications

IS THERE NO DECENCY?

U OF TEXAS – TAYLOR HALL

"I don't know, Professor Smith"
(Pregnant pause) ... "So what you're saying is ..."

U of Texas – Townes Law

STUDYING IS ENLIGHTENING.

TEXAS TECH – LIBRARY

SWEET JESUS, IT'S TIME FOR FINAL EXAMS AND I DON'T
KNOW WHAT'S GOING ON.

SMU – FLORENCE HALL

Everything you know is wrong.

Texas Tech – Science

THE QUESTION IS, "WHY?"

– BELOW –

I HOPE NOT, I DIDN'T STUDY THAT SECTION.

SMU – FLORENCE HALL

Finals are a stupid waste of time.

Baylor – Richardson Science

FRESHMAN MIDTERMS 1980—"GO FOR THE CAPILLARY!"

U OF TEXAS – TOWNES LAW

FINALS MAKE ME URINATE.

TEXAS A&M – AGRICULTURE BUILDING

Finals promote heart problems and brain damage.

Baylor – Hankamer School of Business

(WRITTEN ON PIECE OF TOILET PAPER THUMBTACKED ON INSIDE OF STALL DOOR) GOOD LUCK ON FINALS!

U OF TEXAS – BUSINESS/ECONOMICS

That final was a son-of-a-bitch!

Texas Tech – Chemistry

THE ONLY GOOD FINAL IS A COMPLETED FINAL.

U OF TEXAS – BUSINESS/ECONOMICS

**NO FINALS, NO PAIN
NO PAIN, NO GAIN.**

U OF TEXAS – COCKERALL HALL

Frats are like flies —
they eat shit and
bother people!

ARKANSAS – BUSINESS
ADMINISTRATION

Fraternities and sororities play an active part at most schools in the Southwest Conference, and much is written about these beloved institutions.

Of the ten most disgusting things I know, frat rats are all of them.

Texas Tech – Library

A FRAT IS A FART THAT CAN'T SPELL.

U OF TEXAS – MOORE HALL

IF YOU AIN'T GREEK, YOU AIN'T WORTH SHIT.
TEXAS CHRISTIAN –
RICHARDSON BUILDING

Draft frats, not people!
U of Texas – Undergraduate
Library

EVERYONE IS JEALOUS OF FRATS.

– BELOW –

OF A FRAT RAT'S ABILITY TO WALK AND THINK AT THE SAME TIME.
U OF TEXAS –
BUSINESS/ECONOMICS

I SPAT ON A FRAT.
U OF TEXAS –
BUSINESS/ECONOMICS

Sor-whores and frat-rats all look alike to me, and I'm 100% WASP.
U of Texas – Undergraduate Library

IF BRAINS WERE COTTON, FRAT RATS WOULD NOT HAVE ENOUGH TO KOTEX AN ANT.
TEXAS TECH – LIBRARY

Frat Ratz Suck!

SMU – Fincher Building

IF FRATS DON'T WANT TO BE THOUGHT OF AS FAGS, WHY DON'T THEY STOP DOING ALL THOSE FAG THINGS?

U OF TEXAS – BUSINESS/ECONOMICS

FRAT BOY, FRAT BOY, DON'T BE BLUE JUST BECAUSE YOU HAVE A LOW IQ.

U OF TEXAS – UNDERGRADUATE LIBRARY

Phi Delta—man's best friend.

Texas Tech – Science

HOW TO KEEP PHI DELTS BUSY:
1. PENTHOUSE
2. MAGNIFYING GLASS
3. PAIR OF TWEEZERS.

ARKANSAS – WATERMAN HALL

You can't spell turkey without TKE.

Arkansas – Science/Engineering

IF GREEKS DON'T WANT NO FREAKS, THEN US FREAKS DON'T WANT NO GREEKS.

U OF TEXAS – BUSINESS/ECONOMICS

For you newcomers to the Southwest who find yourselves with weighty problems and no one to turn to—fear not. Numerous counseling programs have been initiated to help out. One example is this advice-giving forum developed in Waterman Hall at the Law School at the University of Arkansas. No question goes unanswered.

Dear Zorro: Why is the universe expanding?

—Confused

Dear Confused: Everything is relative. Actually, you are getting smaller.

—Zorro

DEAR ZORRO: WHY DOES SUPERMAN USE A TELEPHONE BOOTH TO CHANGE TO HIS SECRET IDENTITY AND YOU USE A BATHROOM STALL?

—CONFUSED

DEAR CONFUSED: ALL THAT I AM ALLOWED TO TELL YOU IS THAT SUPERMAN HAS PHONEY REASONS AND I HAVE SHITTY ONES.

—ZORRO

Dear Zorro: My girl friend is ugly, but refuses to let me put a bag over her head when we fuck. What shall I do?

—Confused

Dear Confused: Put a bag over your head.

—Zorro

DEAR ZORRO: WHAT DO YOU CALL IT WHEN YOU LOSE?

—CONFUSED

DEAR CONFUSED: I CALL IT HER TURN TO BE ON TOP.

—ZORRO

DEAR ZORRO: YOU CALL THAT A LOSS?

—CONFUSED

DEAR CONFUSED: NO, SHE'S JUST HEAVY.

—ZORRO

DEAR ZORRO: I JUST GOT BACK FROM SPRING BREAK. I DIDN'T GET DRUNK OR RAPE ANY WOMEN. WHAT'S MY PROBLEM?

—CONFUSED

DEAR CONFUSED: YOU'RE JUST A YANKEE QUEER.

—ZORRO

Dear Zorro: What's the difference between a doctor and a lawyer?

—Uncertain

Dear Uncertain: The difference is between having a job and needing one.

—Zorro

DEAR ZORRO: WHAT IS THE DIFFERENCE BETWEEN A 1ST YEAR LAW STUDENT AND SOMEONE WHO HAS PASSED THE BAR?

—CONFUSED

DEAR CONFUSED: A 1ST YEAR LAW STUDENT NEVER PASSES ANY BAR, DISCO OR LIQUOR STORE. A PERSON WHO HAS PASSED THE BAR GOES TO A HIGHER CLASS ESTABLISHMENT.

—ZORRO

Dear Zorro: Is it true? Is there life after Law School?

—Terminal Law Student

Dear Terminal Law Student: Even though a person's body can be kept running, a person is considered dead when the brain cannot function and cannot be repaired. There is no life after Law School.

—Zorro

Now is the time for some deep thinking on the nature of reality.

ARKANSAS –
SCIENCE/ENGINEERING

If Zorro is unavailable, others will happily provide you with bits of wisdom.

A LIFETIME TO ETERNITY IS LIKE AN ATOM TO THE UNIVERSE.

TEXAS A&M – TEAGUE RESEARCH
CENTER

The stars are matter.
We are matter.
But it doesn't matter.

Arkansas – Chemistry Building

NOTHING MATTERS, BUT EVERYTHING COUNTS.

HOUSTON – LIBRARY

The most difficult thing to know in life is yourself.

U of Texas – Business/Economics

BE AT PEACE WITH YOURSELF, CELEBRATE LIFE.

ARKANSAS – WATERMAN HALL

LIFE GROWS ON THE SIDE OF THE MOUNTAIN, NOT THE TOP.

U OF TEXAS –
BUSINESS/ECONOMICS

Error is half truth.

U of Texas – Moore Hall

THE UNDISCERNING MIND, LIKE A TREE, ABSORBS ALL THAT IT COMES IN CONTACT WITH, INCLUDING THAT SUBSTANCE THAT MIGHT KILL IT.

TEXAS A&M – TEAGUE
RESEARCH CENTER

When wise men act foolishly, then fools may be wise.

U of Texas – Townes Law

*THERE ARE TWO KINDS OF PEOPLE IN THE WORLD—
THOSE WHO DIVIDE THE WORLD INTO TWO KINDS OF
PEOPLE AND THOSE WHO DON'T.*

U OF TEXAS – TOWNES LAW

**FREE MEN ARE NEVER EQUAL. EQUAL MEN ARE NEVER
FREE.**

TEXAS TECH – FAT DAWG'S

If you choose not to decide, you still have made a choice.

U of Texas – Engineering & Science

FIND A JOB YOU LIKE, NOT ONE YOU THINK
SOMEONE ELSE WOULD LIKE.

ARKANSAS – WATERMAN HALL

The only problem with the world today is greed.

Texas Tech – Holden Hall

*THE WHITE MAN DREW TWO CIRCLES, ONE INSIDE
THE OTHER. POINTING TO THE INNER CIRCLE, HE SAID,
"THIS IS HOW MUCH THE INDIAN KNOWS." AND POINTING
TO THE OUTER CIRCLE, HE SAID, "AND THIS IS HOW MUCH
THE WHITE MAN KNOWS." THEN THE INDIAN, POINTING
TO THE AREA OUTSIDE BOTH THE CIRCLES, SAID, "AND
THIS IS WHAT WE BOTH DON'T KNOW."*

*U OF TEXAS – UNDERGRADUATE
LIBRARY*

Life is like a fart —
you hold on to it the best you can,
and when you least expect it,
it slips away.

TEXAS A&M – SCOATES HALL

Newcomers will want to note carefully the nature of life in the Southwest.

LIFE IS LIKE GOING TO THE TOILET—IF IT WEREN'T FOR ITS OCCASIONAL NECESSITY YOU WOULD PROBABLY STILL DO IT OUT OF HABIT.

HOUSTON – SCIENCE BUILDING

Life is like a shit sandwich—the more bread you have, the less shit you have to eat.

Classic on all campuses

LIFE IS A CRAPPER WALL!

TEXAS A&M – OCEANOGRAPHY
& METEOROLOGY

Life is like a beer.

– below –

Life is like a dick, long and hard.

– below –

Life is like sitting here: little surprises keep dropping out
and in the end you get wiped out.

Texas Tech – English

LIFE IS A BITCH AND I AM ITS PUPPY.

U OF TEXAS – CALHOUN HALL

**LIFE'S A TWO-BIT WHORE AND I DON'T HAVE A
QUARTER.**

TEXAS TECH – HOLDEN HALL

Life straight—
Straight bourbon—
Both need a little chaser.

U of Texas – Battle Hall

LIFE IS LIKE A BED OF ROSES—EVERY TIME YOU
MAKE A MOVE, SOMEONE IS STICKING YOU IN THE ASS.

TEXAS A&M – DOGHERTY HALL

Life is a phallic and we are all symbols.

Arkansas – Physics

LIFE IS LIKE A PENIS. WHEN IT'S SOFT, YOU CAN'T BEAT IT. WHEN IT'S HARD, YOU GET SCREWED.

CLASSIC ON ALL CAMPUSES

LIFE IS LIKE PINBALL—YOU HAVE TO SCORE SOME POINTS OR LOSE YOUR BALLS.

HOUSTON – FINE ARTS

What's the meaning of life?

– below –

It's a grand illusion.

– below –

My illusion is killing me.

U of Texas – Welch Hall

WHAT IS LIFE?

– BELOW –

THE KIND OF CEREAL THAT MIKEY LIKES.

TEXAS A&M –
HYDROMECHANICS LAB

God is alive and autographing Bibles, today only, at Hempil's Bookstore.

U OF TEXAS – WOOLRICH HALL

Whether autographing Bibles or busy with other activities, God is not forgotten in the Southwest Conference.

God is good!

– below –

God is the greatest!

U of Texas – Pharmacy

GOD IS ALIVE AND WELL.

– BELOW –

. . . AND APPARENTLY ON VACATION.

BAYLOR – RICHARDSON SCIENCE

God didn't create the world in six days. He rested for five and then crammed.

U of Texas – Moore Hall

GOD GAVE US A WORLD THAT WE ARE MANAGING TO FUCK UP.

U OF TEXAS – TOWNES LAW

'GOD IS A CONCEPT BY WHICH WE MEASURE OUR PAIN.'—JOHN LENNON

– BELOW –

'PAIN IS A CONCEPT ABOUT WHICH JOHN LENNON SAID VERY MUCH AND DID VERY LITTLE.'—GOD

ARKANSAS – CHEMISTRY
BUILDING

Your body is the temple of God. Keep it clean and Holy. And turn out the lights when you leave.

Texas A&M – Heep Building

RADIATION LEAKS ARE MADE BY FOOLS LIKE ME,
BUT ONLY GOD CAN MAKE A NUCLEAR REACTOR THAT
IS 93 MILLION MILES FROM THE NEIGHBORHOOD
ELEMENTARY SCHOOL.

U OF TEXAS – TAYLOR HALL

The fool says in his heart, "There is no God."

Houston – Fine Arts

*REPENT OF YOUR SINS AND ACCEPT CHRIST AS YOUR
SAVIOR, FOR NO MAN KNOWS WHAT TOMORROW MIGHT
BRING. ETERNITY IS FOREVER. WHERE WILL YOU SPEND
YOUR ETERNITY?*

– BELOW –

AKRON, OHIO

*HOUSTON – TECHNOLOGY
ANNEX*

**JESUS MAKES THE DIFFIDENT SWELL UP WITH SELF-
RIGHTEOUSNESS.**

ARKANSAS – AGRICULTURE

Jesus was a wino!

– below –

That is why He was always turning water into wine. Thus was
begat the song "What a friend we have in Jesus."

Texas A&M – Heep Building

THEY DON'T MAKE JEWS LIKE JESUS ANYMORE.

U OF TEXAS –
BUSINESS/ECONOMICS

Before Christ, no one knew.
During Christ, no one believed.
After Christ, no one cared.

Texas A&M – Teague Research
Center

BAPTISTS ARE LIKE CATS—YOU KNOW THEY RAISE
HELL, BUT YOU CAN'T CATCH THEM AT IT.

TEXAS A&M – TEAGUE
RESEARCH CENTER

AND YOU CALL YOURSELVES CHRISTIANS?

TEXAS CHRISTIAN – STUDENT
CENTER

How would all you students like to repent.

U of Texas – Undergraduate Library

THINK HEAVEN!

HOUSTON – HEYNE BUILDING

Love your enemies and pray for those who despitefully
use you.

Texas Christian – Winton Scott
Hall

54

JUDGE NOT THAT YE BE NOT JUDGED.
                          TEXAS TECH – LIBRARY

**LOVE YOUR ENEMIES AND BLESS THOSE WHO PERSECUTE
YOU. IF YOU LOVE ONLY THOSE WHO LOVE YOU, WHAT
CREDIT IS THAT TO YOU?**
                          HOUSTON – CULLEN BUILDING

Read Daniel, Chapters 2 and 3, and Revelations, Chapter 17,
and you'll know the future of the European Common Market and
the world. But read it before it's too late.
                          Texas Christian – Dan Rogers Hall

TRUST IN GOD, HE HAS THE ANSWER.

– BELOW –

THEN WHY DIDN'T HE ANSWER MY HISTORY FINAL?
                          TEXAS TECH – HOLDEN HALL

**I'm so glad that I go to a fine Christian school so that I
can read restroom walls.**
                          Baylor – Richardson Science

DOES GOD CARE THAT I DIDN'T GO TO BAYLOR?
                          U OF TEXAS – MOORE HALL

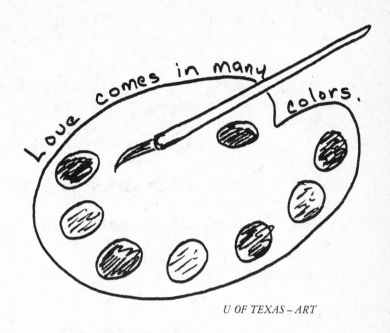

U OF TEXAS – ART

One thing that makes Southwest Conference students happy is other Southwest Conference students.

You know I love the lady's love.

Texas Tech – Art

I LOVE LIZ, NO MATTER WHAT THEY SAY.

U OF TEXAS –

BUSINESS/ECONOMICS

LONE STAR BEER AND BOB WILLS MUSIC HAVE KEPT MY HEART ALIVE SINCE SHE'S BEEN GONE.

HOUSTON – ENGINEERING

56

Love me.

– below –

Give me a chance, like how to contact you.

(phone booth)
U of Texas – Art Building

I THINK THAT W.W. IS THE SEXIEST AND SWEETEST GUY AT RICE. AND I WOULD DEFINITELY LIKE TO SPEND AN EVENING ALONE WITH HIM. PLEASE TELL HIM I'M HIS FAITHFUL ADMIRER.

RICE – LIBRARY

I love Charles.

– below –

Your probably too immature to know what love is, exemplified by your writing on the wall.

– below –

And you are probably too immature to spell "you're" instead of "your."

U of Texas – Art Building

LOVE CANNOT BE DEFINED IN A SINGLE WORD.
HOUSTON – SCIENCE

LOVE IS ALL YOU NEED, EXCEPT FOR MONEY.

–BELOW–

AND FOOD

–BELOW–

AND PUSSY

–BELOW–

A BOAT

–BELOW–

CAR

–BELOW–

C.B.

–BELOW–

MOTOR HOME

–BELOW–

PLACE ON THE LAKE

–BELOW–

DRUGS

–BELOW–

ROCK 'N ROLL

– BELOW –

MOM

– BELOW –

APPLE PIE

– BELOW –

WARM PLACE TO SHIT

– BELOW –

LOOSE SHOES

U OF TEXAS – WAGGENER HALL

There is a vas differens between men and women.

Arkansas – Chemistry Building

WOMEN ARE THE FOUNDATION OF THE WORLD—
JUST REMEMBER WHO LAID THE FOUNDATION.

BAYLOR – MARRS MCLEAN
SCIENCE

Man is like shit, but Woman still likes him.

Texas Tech – Civil & Mechanical
Engineering

ADAM WAS A ROUGH DRAFT.

– BELOW –

WHEN DO WE GET TO SEE THE FINAL MALE COPY?

– BELOW –

I THINK IT'S EVOLVED AS FAR AS IT CAN GO.
                                        RICE – GEOLOGY

A WOMAN WITHOUT A MAN IS LIKE A FISH WITHOUT A BICYCLE.

– BELOW –

LOOK AT THE LEGS ON THAT FISH!
                                        U OF TEXAS – TOWNES LAW

I've about had it with males. Become a lesbian or a nun. Perhaps both.

– below –

Actually, I'd rather be a lesbian.

                    U of Texas – Graduate School of Business

DROP OUT AND GET MARRIED.

                    U OF TEXAS – GRADUATE SCHOOL OF BUSINESS

Always marry an ugly girl—that way she'll never leave you, or if she does, you won't mind.

Texas A&M – Teague Research Center

QUIT LETTING YOUR MEN FUCK YOU AND WE'LL HAVE A BETTER WORLD. REMEMBER LYSISTRATA. WE HAVE POWER IN OUR CUNTS AND WE GIVE IT AWAY. BESIDES, FUCKING CAUSES CERVICAL CANCER.

– BELOW –

STATISTICS ALSO SHOW CIRCUMCIZED MEN CAUSE LESS CANCER, SO FIND A NICE JEWISH BOY.

– BELOW –

THEY'RE THE BEST. I KNOW—I'VE FUCKED THEM ALL.

U OF TEXAS – UNDERGRADUATE LIBRARY

ADULTERY IS BEST!

– BELOW –

ONLY IF YOU'RE AN ADULT.

ARKANSAS – PHYSICS

Alimony is the screwing you get for the screwing you got.

Arkansas – Physics

Candy's dandy...

but sex won't rot your teeth.

TEXAS A&M – FRANCIS HALL

Students in the Southwest Conference appear quick to pursue life's healthier activities.

Love is a four-letter word, but sex isn't.

U of Texas – Geology

SEX IS GREAT!

TEXAS TECH – LIBRARY

CONSERVE ENERGY—HOLD SOMEONE TILL YOU GET WARM.

HOUSTON – FLEMING BUILDING

Help me make it through the night.

Houston – Fleming Building

BEAM ME A BROAD, SCOTTIE!

TEXAS A&M – HEEP BUILDING

For a good time, call 555-7777.

– below –

How good?

– below –

For me, time makes no difference.

Houston – Heyne Building

FOR A GOOD TIME, CALL SPCA.

– BELOW –

I DID, BUT THEY WERE A BUNCH OF REAL DOGS.

HOUSTON – LIBRARY

PLEASE KNOCK SOFTLY BUT FIRMLY, I LIKE SOFT, FIRM KNOCKERS.

U OF TEXAS –

BUSINESS/ECONOMICS

Fondle me!

Texas Tech –Library

I'M SURE HE FELT HER ALRIGHT AT HOME.

U OF TEXAS – MOORE HALL

He who goes out with a flat-chested girl has a right to feel low down.

Texas A&M – Evans Library

STIMULATE CLITORIS!

TEXAS CHRISTIAN – WINTON SCOTT HALL

WOMAN (WU ́ - MAN): A LIFE SUPPORT SYSTEM FOR A VAGINA.

TEXAS A&M – TEAGUE RESEARCH CENTER

Where's a mermaid's cunt?

Texas Tech – Art

QUESTION: WHAT DO GIRLS AND AIRPLANES HAVE IN COMMON?
ANSWER: A COCKPIT.

HOUSTON – SCIENCE BUILDING

64

Country.

– below –

Cunt tree.

– below –

Pussy plant.

– below –

Fertilize!

Texas Tech – Science

SIT ON MY ROOT!

U OF TEXAS – WELCH HALL

I WANT SOME PUSSY!

TEXAS TECH – JOURNALISM

Ashes to ashes.
Dust to dust.
If it weren't for pussy
my dick would rust.

Texas A&M – Scoates Hall

FRESH PUSSY EACH DAY KEEPS THE DOCTOR AWAY.

*U OF TEXAS – WINSHIP DRAMA
BUILDING*

Rice women are bearded tacos.

– below –

Sauce daily.

Rice – Library

WITH LUCK I'LL BE CUMMING TONIGHT.
RICE – GEOLOGY

LAST SPERM IN IS A ROTTEN EGG!
TEXAS A&M – TEAGUE RESEARCH
CENTER

Last night I had sex.
It was good.

Rice – Library

YOU PEOPLE ARE FUCKED.

– BELOW –

YES, SEX DOES PLAY A PART IN MOST OF OUR LIVES.
ARE YOU TRYING TO SAY THAT YOU ARE SEXLESS OR A
PRUDE OR BOTH?

TEXAS TECH – ART

Maximum sex!

Houston – Science Building

I SCREWED SIXTY-SIX GIRLS LAST SUMMER.

– BELOW –

UHUH . . . .

*TEXAS A&M – HELDENFELS
HALL*

IT'S NOT QUANTITY, BUT QUALITY THAT COUNTS.

– BELOW –

**SOMETIMES YOU HAVE TO HAVE QUANTITY TO GET
QUALITY.**

TEXAS TECH – ART

How do you fuck a 600 lb. woman?

– below –

Cautiously.

– below –

On top, for sure.

U of Texas – Moore Hall

MET THE PERFECT WOMAN, SHE'S DEAF, DUMB,
LOVES TO FUCK, AND OWNS A LIQUOR STORE.

CLASSIC ON ALL CAMPUSES

$$\frac{\text{sex}}{\text{vert}} = 1 \text{ sex per vert}$$

U of Texas – Moore Hall

HAVE YOU EVER CONSIDERED THE GEOMETRICAL POSSIBILITIES OF SNOW WHITE AND THE SEVEN DWARFS?

– BELOW –

NO, PERVERT!

– BELOW –

YOU LADIES ARE SO INTOLERANT. PLEASE TRY TO RELAX.

U OF TEXAS – JESTER CENTER

HE WHO FUCKS NUNS WILL LATER JOIN THE CHURCH.

*HOUSTON – ART &
ARCHITECTURE*

Whores are like welders, always hollerin' for more heat, more rods and more money.

Houston – Science Building

Panty hose are all show and no go.

U of Texas – Moore Hall

No fuck for you, Lady!

RICE – BIOLOGY

VIRGINITY IS LIKE A BALLOON, ONE PRICK AND IT'S GONE.

TEXAS TECH – LIBRARY

A GIRL'S BEST FRIEND IS HER LEGS.

HOUSTON – HEYNE BUILDING

Bow-legged women stay on longer.

Texas A&M – Teague Research Center

ART MAJORS DO IT WITH THEIR BRUSHES.

HOUSTON – FINE ARTS

Pole vaulters get higher.

U of Texas – Winship Drama Building

TROMBONISTS DO IT IN ANY POSITION.
                    HOUSTON – FINE ARTS

AGGIES DO IT BETTER.

– BELOW –

WILDLIFE BIOLOGISTS DO IT LIKE ANIMALS.

– BELOW –

FARMERS DO IT IN THE DIRT.

– BELOW –

WELDERS DO IT WITH BIGGER RODS.

– BELOW –

WELL DIGGERS DO IT DEEPER.
                    TEXAS A&M – SCOATES HALL

Bass players get down.
                    Houston – Fine Arts

DO IT IN A TUBA!
                    HOUSTON – FINE ARTS

A cowboy don't care how he fills out his pants. He just cares how it feels when it's hard.
                    Houston – Arnold Auditoria

QUESTION: HOW DO I MAKE IT 10"?
ANSWER: FOLD IT IN HALF.

U OF TEXAS – MOORE HALL

YOUR PETER IS THE ONLY THING THE GOVERNMENT CAN'T TAX.

– BELOW –

I PAY A POLE TAX ON MINE.

– BELOW –

PLEASE, NO JOKES, SOME OF MY BEST FRIENDS ARE POLES.

TEXAS A&M – TEAGUE RESEARCH CENTER

Question: What has twenty-seven teeth and holds back the Incredible Hulk?
Answer: My zipper.

Texas A&M – Teague Research Center

MY BALLS FEEL LIKE A PAIR OF MORACCAS.

TEXAS TECH – ENGLISH

Has anyone ever told you that you're hung like a hamster?

SMU – Fincher Memorial Building

IT WAS I THAT DID THE PUSHIN'
LEFT THE STAINS UPON THE CUSHIN'
AND MY FOOTPRINTS ON THE DASHBOARD UPSIDE
DOWN.
BUT SINCE I SCREWED YOUR DAUGHTER
I'VE HAD TROUBLE PASSIN' WATER,
SO NOW I THINK WE'RE EVEN ALL AROUND.

U OF TEXAS – GEOLOGY

SORES ON THE DORK AGAIN?

U OF TEXAS – MOORE HALL

With regard to landslides, even a mountain has to get its rocks off now and then.

Rice – Geology

LOCALIZED THRUSTING WILL CAUSE DYNAMIC METAMORPHISM OF LOCAL CUNTRY ROCK.

RICE – KEITH WEISS
GEOLOGICAL LABS

Thrust and uplift are common in zones of orogeny.

Rice – Geology

Help the farmer...

eat pussy, not beef.

TEXAS A&M – ANALYTICAL SCIENCES

Southwest Conference students are always anxious to help out the less fortunate.

JOIN THE CRUSADE TO SAVE THE MICE! EAT A PUSSY EVERY DAY!

TEXAS CHRISTIAN – DAN ROGERS HALL

I would like to eat a pussy!

– below –

Eat yourself then.

– below –

I think he means a different pussy.

Arkansas – Business Administration

I SNATCH KISSES AND VICE VERSA.

TEXAS A&M – TEAGUE
RESEARCH CENTER

Some people say that pussy tastes like anchovies. I wouldn't know about that, I've never eaten anchovies.

Arkansas – Chemistry

ALL OF US MEN DOWN ON OUR KNEES
CAN EAT MORE PUSSY THAN A RAT CAN CHEESE.

TEXAS TECH – HOLDEN HALL

SIT ON A HAPPY FACE.

TEXAS TECH – HOLDEN HALL

How can I get her off my mind when she's sitting on my face?

U of Texas – Business/Economics

SPANK YOUR HONEY TONIGHT.

– BELOW –

HELL, I GAVE HER A GOOD LICKIN' LAST NIGHT.

U OF TEXAS – PAINTER HALL

What in hell is a jabberwock?

– below –

A good head job in German.

U of Texas – Moore Hall

99% OF COLLEGE COEDS GIVE HEAD.
THE OTHER 1% GO TO TCU.

TEXAS CHRISTIAN –
RICHARDSON BUILDING

IF I COULD BLOW MYSELF, I WOULDN'T LEAVE THE HOUSE.

(OLD COLORADO ADAGE)
TEXAS CHRISTIAN – SADLER
ADMINISTRATION

*Masturbation —
the art of coming unscrewed.*

SMU – Fincher Building

Self-reliance is an admired characteristic among students of the Southwest Conference.

GIVE ME A ROSIE, OR GIVE ME HAND!

SMU – FINCHER BUILDING

**Pussy is sweet.
So is money.
Beat your meat
and save the money.**

Rice – Memorial Center

EXPERIENCE THE JOY OF BOTH GIVING AND RECEIVING—BEAT OFF.

RICE – RAYZOR HALL

IF YOU SHAKE MORE THAN ONCE, YOU'RE PLAYING WITH IT.

U OF TEXAS – WINSHIP DRAMA BUILDING

The guy next to you is spanking his monkey.

Texas Tech – Fat Dawg's

RUBBIN' THE NUBBIN.

–BELOW –

SHOOTIN' THE HOOTER.

– BELOW –

JERKIN' THE BEEF.

– BELOW –

DRAININ' THE LIZARD.

TEXAS A&M – TEAGUE RESEARCH CENTER

Beware of jerking commode!

U of Texas – Business/Economics

BENEATH THE SPREADING CHESTNUT TREE
THE VILLAGE IDIOT SAT,
AMUSING HIMSELF
BY ABUSING HIMSELF
AND CATCHING IT IN HIS HAT.

HOUSTON – SCIENCE BUILDING

HI, HO. HI, HO.
IT'S OFF TO WORK WE GO.
FIRST WE JERK,
AND THEN WE WORK.
HI, HO. HI, HO.

RICE – KEITH WEISS
GEOLOGICAL LABS

When I was young and in my prime,
I jacked off almost all the time.
Now I'm older, got more sense,
and use the knot hole in the fence.

Texas A&M – Oceonography &
Meteorology

Drugs are not
the answer –

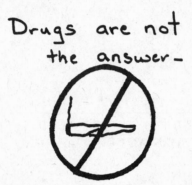

they are merely
a form of the question,

And one finds varying opinion about drugs.

REALITY IS FOR THOSE WHO CAN'T HANDLE DRUGS.
CLASSIC ON ALL CAMPUSES

Reality is a ~~crutch~~ crotch for those who can't handle drugs.
U of Texas – Townes Law

DRUGS ARE FOR PEOPLE WHO CAN'T GET SEX.

– BELOW –

SOCIALLY MALADJUSTED PERSONS TAKE DRUGS.
TEXAS TECH – LIBRARY

Death is a concept by which we measure our drugs.

Arkansas – Science/Engineering

LSD GOT A HOLD ON ME.

RICE – SEWELL HALL

SUPPORT LSD—THE FOURTH NETWORK.

BAYLOR – MARRS MCLEAN
SCIENCE

Acid consumes 47 times its weight in excess reality.

Classic on all campuses

GET STONED!

– BELOW –

BUT DON'T TAKE IT FOR GRANITE.

TEXAS TECH – HOLDEN HALL

Looking out on eternity,
Gazing with tranquility.

Houston – Law

GOD IS PERFECT.
MAN IS NOT.
MAN MADE WHISKEY.
GOD MADE POT.

U OF TEXAS – PAINTER HALL

**JESUS FORGIVES A GOOD HEAD WHO REPEATS,
"I BELIEVE" BETWEEN TOKES.**

RICE – MEMORIAL CENTER

A reefer a day . . . I forgot the rest.

Texas A&M – Scoates Hall

HALLUCINATE DAILY!

RICE – SEWELL HALL

Mushrooms are best.

U of Texas – Geology

MAGIC MUSHROOMS!

*U OF TEXAS – WINSHIP DRAMA
BUILDING*

Rock 'n roll will
send you to Hell!

BAYLOR – MARRS MCLEAN
SCIENCE

Going to the Southwest does not mean giving up rock 'n' roll.

Long live rock 'n roll!

– below –

Jazz too!

Texas Tech – Civil & Mechanical
Engineering

LONG LIVE NON-REPRESENTATIONAL MUSIC!
TEXAS TECH – LIBRARY

THEY SHOT JOHN LENNON, MY MAN.

U OF TEXAS – UNDERGRADUATE
LIBRARY

John Lennon is dead. Is the dream over too?

U of Texas – Business/Economics

LONG LIVE LENNON!

TEXAS TECH – LIBRARY

I guess we won't have a Beatles reunion, eh?

Texas A&M – Harrington Building

DO THE AQUA VELVA!

– BELOW –

SHY TUNA

– BELOW –

HIP-O-CRITE

– BELOW –

DIRTY DOG

– BELOW –

ESCALATOR

– BELOW –

SHAKE-BAKE

– BELOW –

BUC-A-LOO

U OF TEXAS – TOWNES LAW

BETTER DEAD THAN DISCO.

TEXAS A&M – HELDENFELS HALL

Disco is to music what traffic court is to justice.

Texas A&M – Francis Hall

WOULD MOZART HAVE WRITTEN DISCO?

– BELOW –

WOULD SHAKESPEARE HAVE WRITTEN GOTHIC ROMANCES?

HOUSTON – FINE ARTS

Disco is a Communist plot!

Texas A&M – Heldenfels Hall

Bonzo for First Chimp!

U OF TEXAS – WAGGENER HALL

As a newcomer to the Southwest, you will find politics elevated to its proper position.

REAGAN FOR PRESIDENT!

– BELOW –

OH, CRUEL FATE, THY STOUDT SHAFT DOTH ONCE AGAIN ASSAIL THE NATIONAL RECTUM. RUDE! FOUL!

U OF TEXAS – TAYLOR HALL

Reagan beat the shit out of Carter.

Texas Tech – Holden Hall

I WANT TO GET FUCKED.

– BELOW –

YOU DID ON INAUGURATION DAY.

TEXAS TECH – HOLDEN HALL

Billy Jack for President!

– below –

That's who we got.

Texas Tech – Holden Hall

REAGAN AND THE KKK—THE EMBODIMENT OF THE AMERICAN IDEAL.

U OF TEXAS – GRADUATE
SCHOOL OF BUSINESS

IF YOU VOTED FOR REAGAN YOU CAN'T SHIT HERE, YOUR ASSHOLE'S IN WASHINGTON.

TEXAS TECH – CHEMISTRY

I think Reagan's promised me two feet of space in the unemployment line.

U of Texas – Townes Law

RONALD REAGAN WAS HERE, BUT I FLUSHED HIM.

TEXAS A&M – BIOLOGICAL
SCIENCES

Any government that is big enough to give you what you want is big enough to take what you have.

Texas A&M – Architecture Center

STARVATION IS GOD'S WAY OF PUNISHING THOSE WHO HAVE LITTLE OR NO FAITH IN CAPITALISM.

U OF TEXAS – GEOLOGY

UP THE ASS OF THE MIDDLE CLASS!

– BELOW –

BE ORIGINAL.

U OF TEXAS – UNDERGRADUATE LIBRARY

Nerds out of Congress now!

U of Texas – Painter Hall

TEDDY FOR LIFE GUARD!

TEXAS A&M – HELDENFELS HALL

And, Senator Kennedy, what would you do to straighten out the economy?

I'll drive off that bridge when I come to it.

Texas A&M – Heldenfels Hall

We want nukes!
We want war!
We think oil is worth fighting for!

– below –

Paid for by the National Hand Grenade Owner's Association.

Arkansas – Physics

RICE – LIBRARY

NUKE JANITORS!

– BELOW –

NUKE YO MAMMA!

– BELOW –

NUKE ROCKNE!

ARKANSAS –
SCIENCE/ENGINEERING

Go nukes! No kooks!

Texas A&M – Heldenfels Hall

NATIONS ARE A FARCE!

RICE – RAYZOR HALL

I am an American elitist and I have no guilt.

Rice – Library

SEND THE MARINES!

TEXAS TECH – LIBRARY

HEALTHY CONFLICT IS FINE, BUT REMEMBER THERE WILL COME A DAY WHEN YOU'LL BLESS THE ROAR OF AFTER-BURNERS AND PRAISE THE BRAVERY OF FIGHTING SOLDIERS.

ARKANSAS – COMMERCE

I've fucked in Boston. I've fucked in Spain.
I've fucked from Texas to the coast of Maine.
But I'll never be happy and I'll never be free
till I fuck the Army the way they fucked me.

U of Texas – Moore Hall

WHEN I WAS IN THE ARMY THEY GAVE ME A MEDAL FOR KILLING A MAN AND A DISHONORABLE DISCHARGE FOR LOVING ONE.

U OF TEXAS – TOWNES LAW

War is menstruation envy.

U of Texas – Graduate School of Business

Question: What's flat and glows?
Answer: Iran, next week.

– below –

Alternate answer: A lightning bug on your windshield.

Arkansas – Commerce

WHEN YOU PISS, THINK OF IRAN, IT'S EASIER.

SOUTHERN METHODIST –
STOREY HALL

WILL ROGERS NEVER MET AN IRANIAN.

TEXAS A&M – HELDENFELS HALL

Why don't we come right out and tell Iran that we're after their turbans?

U of Texas – Winship Drama Building

ARABS SUCK OIL!

– BELOW –

HOW CRUDE!

HOUSTON – FLEMING BUILDING

Do you think that the oil will last forever?

Southern Methodist – Caruth Hall

That is so funny, I remember the first time I heard it, I laughed so hard my dinosaur damned near bucked me off.

TEXAS A&M – SCOATES HALL

Southwest Conference students are not without their sense of humor.

THAT'S AS FUNNY AS ONE PAY TOILET IN A DIARRHEA WARD.

TEXAS TECH – HOLDEN HALL

Question: What do you call a virgin on a waterbed?
Answer: A cherry float.

Dallas – Fort Worth Airport

90

QUESTION: WHAT DO YOU GET WHEN YOU CROSS A DONKEY WITH AN ONION?
ANSWER: A PIECE OF ASS THAT WILL MAKE YOUR EYES WATER.

BAYLOR – HANKAMER SCHOOL OF BUSINESS

Question: Why did the chicken cross the road?
Answer: He had an easement.

SMU – Florence Hall

QUESTION: WHAT DID MOSES DO WHEN HE FOUND THAT HE HAD ONLY ONE ADDER (SNAKE)?
ANSWER: HE BUILT A TABLE FROM LOGS AND PLACED THE ADDER UPON IT, FOR HE HAD HEARD THAT AN ADDER CAN MULTIPLY ON A LOG TABLE.

ARKANSAS – PHYSICS

DID YOU HEAR ABOUT THE FBI INVESTIGATING YELLOW JOURNALISM IN NEWSPAPERS? THEY CALL IT A PAP SMEAR.

U OF TEXAS – TOWNES LAW

Neil Armstrong tripped.

Texas A&M – Physics Building

CUSTER WORE ARROW SHIRTS.

SMU – FINCHER BUILDING

Armadillo—possum on the half-shell.

U of Texas – Townes Law

WANTED: A HENWAY.
WHAT'S A HENWAY?
OH, ABOUT 6½ POUNDS.

> *U OF TEXAS – WINSHIP DRAMA*
> *BUILDING*

POLYGAMY IS HAVING MORE WIVES THAN YOU NEED.
MONOGAMY IS THE SAME THING.

> *U OF TEXAS –*
> *BUSINESS/ECONOMICS*

The Starship Enterprise's mission—circle around Uranus in search of Clingons.

> *Texas Christian – Richardson Building*

MARY HAD A LITTLE WATCH.
SHE SWALLOWED IT ONE DAY.
SO MARY TOOK SOME CASTOR OIL
TO PASS THE TIME AWAY.

THE CASTOR OIL DIDN'T WORK,
THE PIECE JUST WOULDN'T PASS.
SO IF YOU WANT TO KNOW THE TIME
JUST LOOK UP MARY'S ASS.

> *TEXAS CHRISTIAN –*
> *RICHARDSON BUILDING*

Tommy had a turtle.
Suzy had a duck.
They put them in the bathtub
to see if they would swim.

> *Texas Christian – Landreth Hall*

WE SHOULD ELIMINATE DOUBT, I THINK . . .
HOUSTON – LIBRARY

I'm neither for nor against apathy.
U of Texas – Undergraduate Library

PARANOIDS ARE JUSTIFIED.
TEXAS A&M – SCOATES HALL

Death to fanatics! We will not rest until we see every last fanatic dead!
U of Texas – Painter Hall

I'M NOT A HYPOCHONDRIAC . . . I JUST THINK I AM.
ARKANSAS – PSYCHOLOGY

TO BE IS TO DO — NIETZSCHE
TO DO IS TO BE — SARTRE
DO BE DO BE DO — SINATRA
YABBA DABBA DO — FRED FLINTSTONE
DO BEE A DO BEE — ROMPER ROOM
U OF TEXAS – TOWNES LAW

Creators unite! All you have to lose is your creatures.
Arkansas – Memorial Hall

DOES THE NAME PAVLOV RING A BELL?

– BELOW –

WHAT ABOUT QUASIMODO?

– BELOW –

I HAD A HUNCH HE WAS BACK.

U OF TEXAS – TOWNES LAW

Procrastinators club may meet in five years.

Arkansas – Physics

Step into the reading room.

TEXAS TECH – HOLDEN HALL

Southwest graffitiists find a great deal to write about the activities pursued in their favorite depository of ink.

HAVE A SEAT, WE'LL BE WITH YOU IN A MINUTE.

HOUSTON – TECHNOLOGY
ANNEX

Petition:
Subject: taller stools

Texas Tech – Science

PLEASE STAY SEATED FOR THE HOLE PERFORMANCE.

SMU – FINCHER BUILDING

98

This sure is a small pot.

– below –

As compared to what?

Texas Tech – Science

I DREAMT I DWELT IN MARBLE WALLS,
AND WOKE TO FIND IT TRUE.
I WASN'T BORN FOR AN AGE LIKE THIS,
WAS SMITH? WAS JONES? WERE YOU?

RICE – RAYZOR HALL

PLEASE SHIT RESPECTFULLY—YOU ARE IN ARKANSAS'
FOUNTAIN OF INTELLIGENCE.

ARKANSAS – WATERMAN HALL

Occupancy of this stall by more than two people is disgusting
and illegal.

Rice – Geology

DON'T MIND ME, I'M ONLY HERE TO OBSERVE.

ARKANSAS – MEMORIAL HALL

I don't understand, it's been my birthday every time that
I've been in here.

Texas Christian – Richardson
Building

CRAPPER DOOR, WHY DO YOU STARE AT ME?
U OF TEXAS – ENGINEERING
SCIENCE

I SHUT THE DOOR BECAUSE I'M A MEANIE.
I LIKE MY PRIVACY WHILE I WIPE MY KHOMEINI.
TEXAS CHRISTIAN – DAN ROGERS
HALL

Cut the crap! Cut the budget!

– below –

Cut both, just don't cut the cheese.
Baylor – Richardson Science

IF YOU'VE COME TO TAKE A SHIT, YOU'RE IN LUCK, I
LEFT ONE OF MINE FOR YOU.
ARKANSAS –
SCIENCE/ENGINEERING
BUILDING

If you took a shit here, please return it—no questions
asked.
Texas Tech – Holden Hall

WHO EVER TOOK A SHIT HERE ON MONDAY, PLEASE
RETURN IT.

– BELOW –

I LOST IT IN A POKER GAME.

ARKANSAS – CHEMISTRY
BUILDING

GET YOUR REVENGE; SHIT ON A PIGEON TODAY.

TEXAS A&M – CONFERENCE
CENTER

Please write weight down so that if you fall in we will know how much shit to shovel out.

Texas Christian – Richardson Building

GRUNT WHEN YOU SHIT; IT RELEASES LIBIDO.

ARKANSAS – MEMORIAL
BUILDING

If shit were deemed of value, poor people would be born without assholes.

Texas A&M – Teague Research
Center

ONE HUNDRED TRILLION FLIES CAN'T BE WRONG; EAT SHIT!

– BELOW –

THAT'S WHY THEY DIE SO QUICKLY, TWIT!

TEXAS TECH – HOLDEN HALL

CAN YOU HEAT-TREAT SHIT?

ARKANSAS – MECHANICAL
ENGINEERING

Ashes to ashes,
dust to dust,
if it weren't for your asshole
your belly would bust.

U of Texas – Townes Law

T.S. ELLIOT SAT HERE, BUT I FLUSHED HIM DOWN
TO THE WASTELAND.

RICE – RAYZOR HALL

See? You didn't have to shit after all.

Texas A&M – Teague Research
Center

MAN'S NEED TO SHIT—INALIENABLE.

U OF TEXAS – MOORE HALL

**UNIFORMITY: YOU SHIT TODAY, SO YOU WILL SURELY
SHIT TOMORROW.**

TEXAS TECH – SCIENCE

Flush twice, it's a long way to the cafeteria.

Classic on all campuses

THE SEAT YOU ARE SITTING ON WILL SELF-DESTRUCT IN 1.5 MINUTES AFTER USE.

TEXAS TECH – ART

In five seconds this stall will self-destruct and make your mission impossible.

U of Texas – Moore Hall

HEY, I'M NEW AROUND HERE, COULD SOMEONE TELL ME WHERE THE TOILET PAPER IS?

– BELOW –

TURN YOUR HEAD 180° AND LOOK AT THE OTHER SIDE OF THE STALL.

ARKANSAS – VOL WALKER HALL

HOUSTON – TECHNOLOGY ANNEX

This toilet paper will tear on any line but the perforated one.

U of Texas – Townes Law

(REFERRING TO TOILET PAPER)
IS THIS 20TH CENTURY ENGINEERING?

– BELOW –

YEP, JUST LIKE THE ASTRONAUTS USED.

RICE – RAYZOR HALL

This paper is guaranteed to reduce your hemorrhoids by the sandpaper method.

Arkansas – Physics

THIS TOILET PAPER IS LIKE JOHN WAYNE—IT DON'T TAKE SHIT OFF ANYBODY.

Texas A&M – Heldenfels Hall

DO YOU WAD OR FOLD YOUR TOILET PAPER? THE PSYCH DEPARTMENT KNOWS.

ARKANSAS – MEMORIAL HALL

If the toilet paper runs out, fear not—the afternoon Battalion is out.

Texas A&M – Teague Research Center

DON'T LOOK HERE, THE JOKE'S BETWEEN YOUR LEGS.

CLASSIC ON ALL CAMPUSES

If you can piss above this line, the Fire Department needs you.

Texas Christian – Winton Scott Hall

*NO MATTER HOW YOU WIGGLE AND DANCE,
THE LAST DROPS ALWAYS FALL IN YOUR PANTS.*

CLASSIC ON ALL CAMPUSES

**YOU CAN SHAKE IT TILL IT HURTS.
YOU CAN BEAT IT ON THE WALL.
BUT YOU GOT TO PUT IT IN YOUR PANTS
TO MAKE THE LAST DROP FALL.**

U OF TEXAS – TAYLOR HALL

Our aim is to keep this bathroom clean.
Your aim will help.

– below –

In case of attack, hide under the toilets, they never get hit.

Rice – Library

PISS ON THE FLOOR, NOT ON THE SEAT.
I RESPECT MY ASS MORE THAN MY FEET.

TEXAS TECH – HOLDEN HALL

**Be like dad, not like sis,
lift the lid before you piss.**

Classic on all campuses

when I was just a young nipper,
people didn't go around writing things
in the cracks between building tiles.

Rice – Space Science

It appears that most Southwest "nippers," whether young or old, have got into the debate over graffiti.

GRAF—FROM GERMAN, GRAFFEN, MEANING "TO READ"
ITI—FROM LATIN MEANING, "THAT WHICH IS WRITTEN"

TEXAS A&M – TEAGUE
RESEARCH CENTER

Anyone caught writing graffiti will be suspended.
Texas Tech – Holden Hall

THIS WALL IS PROTECTED BY U.S. CONSTITUTION AMENDMENTS I AND XIV.

U OF TEXAS – TOWNES LAW

WALL WRITERS OF THE WORLD, UNITE!

TEXAS A&M – PHYSICS BUILDING

Iggieland—Give us your best graffiti.

Texas A&M – Teague Research Center

SMU SMUT IS BEST!

SMU – FLORENCE HALL

The graffiti at SMU is the worst I've ever seen. SMU students have no sense of humor, of the irrelevant, or of political, social or religious consciousness.

SMU – Florence Hall

THE GRAFFITI AT BAYLOR IS APPALLING!

BAYLOR – MORRISON
CONSTITUTIONAL HALL

THIS WALL IS BLANK . . . ARE THERE NO LITERATE SHITTERS?

RICE – ANDERSON BIO LABS

If people would write intelligent things on bathroom walls there would be no need to go to college.

Texas Tech – Social Science

WHY DOESN'T ANYONE WRITE SOMETHING CREATIVE? I'M GETTING BORED WITH ALL THIS CRAP.

U OF TEXAS – GRADUATE
SCHOOL OF BUSINESS

This is no doubt the most boring graffiti on campus. Come on, girls, show some imagination.

Rice – Biology

KEEP AMERICA LAUGHING, WRITE MORE GRAFFITI.

U OF TEXAS – MOORE HALL

I HAVE NEVER SEEN SUCH NON-CREATIVITY. IT'S DISGUSTING.

ARKANSAS – VOL WALKER HALL

This door is rated "X".

Rice – Geology

PROFANITY IS THE LINGUISTIC CRUTCH OF THE INARTICULATE BASTARDS.

CLASSIC ON ALL CAMPUSES

I am not mad, I would just like to say, "Motherfucker!"

Texas Christian – Landreth Hall

FUCK OFF!

– BELOW –

SUCH ELOQUENCE.

U OF TEXAS – CALHOUN HALL

ALWAYS THE SICKIES!

***TEXAS A&M – ENGINEERING
BUILDING***

(on a much-written-on toilet-paper dispenser)
Could we paint this thing and start over?

Baylor – Morrison Constitution Hall

THE BALL POINT PEN IS MIGHTIER THAN THE
MAGIC MARKER.

RICE – GEOLOGY

How did Man communicate before the stall was invented?

– below –

He dribbled in the sand.

***Texas A&M – Zachary Engineering
Center***

ANTIQUE GRAFFITI NATIONAL MONUMENT.

RICE – ABERCROMBIE LAB

THERE IS NOTHING WORSE THAN A CLICHÉ VANDAL.

U OF TEXAS – WINSHIP DRAMA
BUILDING

To anyone who wants to write the "Little Balls of Shit" poem, you are shit.

Texas Tech – Journalism

PEOPLE WHO WRITE ON SHIT HOUSE WALLS
ROLL THEIR SHIT IN LITTLE BALLS.
PEOPLE WHO READ THOSE WORDS OF WIT
EAT THE LITTLE BALLS OF SHIT.

CLASSIC ON ALL CAMPUSES

Poetic you are not. But I have to give credit where credit is due, and that is that you are mentally very sick.

Arkansas – Communications

PITY THE POET WHO IS INSPIRED BY THE SMELL IN HERE.

TEXAS CHRISTIAN –
RICHARDSON BUILDING

WHEN ALL THE SHITHOUSE POETS DIE
THEY WILL FIND ERECTED IN THE SKY,
IN TRIBUTE TO THEIR MINDLESS WIT,
A MONUMENT OF SOLID SHIT.

ARKANSAS – MECHANICAL
ENGINEERING

I came to sit and shit and say,
"Shithouse poems are here to stay."

U of Texas – Pharmacy

THE ARTIST'S PRIDE MUST GREATLY FALL
TO SHOW HIS WORK ON SHITHOUSE WALLS.

ARKANSAS – AGRICULTURE

I have a cold.

Well, get hot then!

Texas A&M – Architecture Center

(BESIDE PICTURE OF PENIS)
LIMIT: ONE SELF-PORTRAIT PER WALL.

TEXAS A&M – TEAGUE
RESEARCH CENTER

(BESIDE TOILET-PAPER DISPENSER)
A TREE HAD TO DIE FOR YOU TO WIPE.

RICE – SEWELL HALL

(beside toilet-paper dispenser)
Maximum operating speed, 5,000 rpm.

Texas A&M – Conference Center

(BESIDE TOILET-PAPER DISPENSER)
CBS WHITE PAPER.

U OF TEXAS – TAYLOR HALL

(beside toilet-paper dispenser)
A&M Diploma.

U of Texas – Business/Economics

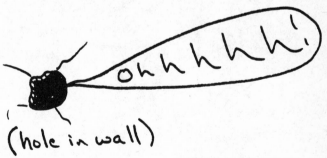

U OF TEXAS – MOORE HALL

(BESIDE HOLE IN STALL DIVIDER)
POWER TO THE PEEP HOLE!

U OF TEXAS – UNDERGRADUATE
LIBRARY

(beside a nickel glued to the inside of a stall wall)
You can't buy anything with a nickel these days.

U of Texas – Battle Hall

UPSIDE DOWN.
IF YOU CAN READ THIS, YOUR EYEBALLS ARE

U OF TEXAS – MOORE HALL

(near area of erasure)
Renderings removed by member of moral majority.

Texas Tech – Art

BAPTISTS ARE COMPULSIVE GRAFFITI ERASERS.
ARKANSAS – AGRICULTURE

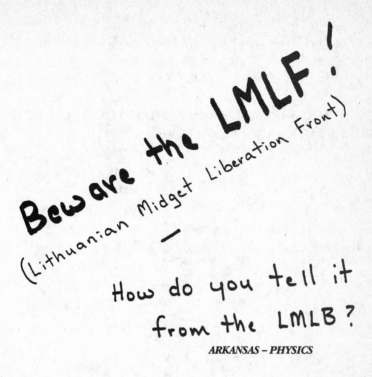

Beware the LMLF!

(Lithuanian Midget Liberation Front)

—

How do you tell it from the LMLB?

ARKANSAS – PHYSICS

If you write graffiti on a wall in the Southwest Conference, be prepared to receive at least one response from a fellow graffitiist.

Call 555 – 7777, ask for Bud.

– below –

This Bud's for you.

Texas Tech – Holden Hall

113

SAVE THE WHALES, DOLPHINS AND BABY SEALS!

– BELOW –

IF YOU SAVE ENOUGH OF THEM YOU CAN TRADE THEM IN FOR LAWN FURNITURE.

U OF TEXAS –
BUSINESS/ECONOMICS

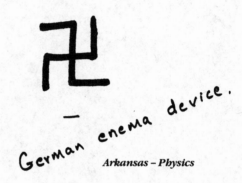

German enema device.

Arkansas – Physics

"ANUS" SPELLED BACKWARDS IS "SUNA", THE JAPANESE WORD FOR RICE.

– BELOW –

COPULATE WITH CORN.

– BELOW –

FLAGELLATE FLAX.

– BELOW –

BALL BARLEY.

RICE – LIBRARY

I NEED A REEFER.

– BELOW –

I ROOF A NEEDER.

– BELOW –

I REEF A NOODER.

– BELOW –

I REEF A NEUTER.

– BELOW –

I KNEED A GOLFER.

– BELOW –

I GOLFED ANITA.

HOUSTON – LAW

Things that I've said more than once:

– below –

It's not the heat, it's the humidity.

– below –

Business is business.

– below –

Boys will be boys.

U of Texas – Graduate School of Business

JESUS SAVES, BUT ESPOSITO SCORES ON REBOUNDS.

– BELOW –

MOHAMMED INVESTS.

– BELOW –

KHOMEINI SPECULATES.

– BELOW –

CARTER DIDDLES.

– BELOW –

HARLEM RAMBLES.

– BELOW –

SPEED KILLS.

– BELOW –

KEED SPILLS.

U OF TEXAS – TOWNES LAW

(in various cracks between tiles)
This cracks me up.

– below –

Jimmy crack corn.

– below –

Krakatoa.

– below –

Cracklin' Rosie.

– below –

Cracker Jack.

– below –

Crack of dawn.

– below –

San Andreas fault.

U of Texas – Townes Law

INVENT A SELF-OPERATIVE STATEMENT. I.E. 1) NOSTALGIA AIN'T WHAT IT USED TO BE. 2) PROFANITY IS THE CRUTCH OF THE INARTICULATE BASTARDS.

– BELOW –

GENERALIZATIONS ARE ALWAYS OVERBLOWN.

– BELOW –

THERE ARE NO EXCEPTIONS TO THE RULE THAT EVERY RULE HAS ITS EXCEPTIONS.

– BELOW –

I HARDLY EVER EQUIVOCATE.

– BELOW –

NIHILISM DOESN'T EXIST.

– BELOW –

NECROPHILIA IS DEAD.

– BELOW –

SOLIPSISM IS A POPULAR DELUSION.

– BELOW –

REDUNDANCIES, THAT IS STATEMENTS THAT REPEAT THEMSELVES, ABOUND. THERE ARE MANY.

– BELOW –

ESCHEW OBFUSCATION.

– BELOW –

WHAT GOOD ARE RHETORICAL QUESTIONS?
U OF TEXAS – TOWNES LAW

I ONCE SPIED A BIRD WHO COULDN'T SING.

– BELOW –

USING 'WHO' IS ANTHROPOMORPHISM (APPLYING HUMAN ATTRIBUTES TO ANIMALS).

– BELOW –

WRONG, NOODLE BRAIN—APPLYING HUMAN ATTRIBUTES TO ANIMALS IS CALLED PERSONIFICATION.

– BELOW –

WRONG AGAIN, SNAKE BREATH—PERSONIFICATION IS A BROAD TERM WHICH ALSO INCLUDES ANY INANIMATE OBJECT.

– BELOW –

SO, THE BIRD WAS DEAD, THEN.

– BELOW –

CONSISTENTLY INCONSISTENT.

– BELOW –

UTTER ELEPHANT SHIT!

– BELOW –

YOU JUST DID.

TEXAS A&M – ENGINEERING
BUILDING

King Kong smokes a bong.

– below –

Sings a song.

– below –

Wiggles his dong.

– below –

Nope, you're wrong.

Texas A&M – Physics Building

LIST THE BIGGEST LIES:

– BELOW –

THE CHECK IS IN THE MAIL.

– BELOW –

I WON'T COME IN YOUR MOUTH.

– BELOW –

OF COURSE I LOVE YOU.

– BELOW –

I LIKE YOUR MOTHER.

– BELOW –

I LIKE YOUR SISTER.

– BELOW –

I'LL ONLY STICK THE HEAD IN.

– BELOW –

I'LL RESPECT YOU IN THE MORNING.

– BELOW –

I'LL WRITE YOU FROM THE CITY.

– BELOW –

I PULLED OUT IN TIME.

– BELOW –

THIS IS MY SECOND TIME.

– BELOW –

I JUST WANT TO LOOK AT IT.

TEXAS TECH – FAT DAWG'S

Write about the phrase "the brown route."

– below –

Refers to that orifice which is increasingly expanded throughout one's first year in Law School.

– below –

The bus route I ride every morning to get here.

– below –

The lower portion of a brown tree.

– below –

Summary of the way California politics went.

– below –

Runs parallel to the yellow brick road.

– below –

Main thoroughfare to Sewer Hole.

Arkansas – Waterman Hall

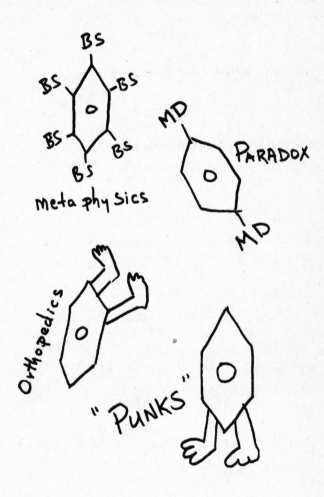

BS

BS — BS

BS — BS

BS — BS

BS

meta phy sics

MD

PARADOX

MD

Orthopedics

"PUNKS"

TEXAS A&M – TEAGUE
RESEARCH CENTER

124

"NOW, CUT THAT OUT." JACK BENNY TO ROCHESTER.

– BELOW –

"AW, GEE, EDDIE, CUT IT OUT." THE BEAVE

– BELOW –

"CUT THAT OUT, ANDY." THE BARN

– BELOW –

"CUT ME." ROCKY

– BELOW –

"CUT ME, BABY." THE FONZ

– BELOW –

"CUT ME SOME SLACK." HAGGAR MEN'S WEAR

– BELOW –

"CUT A RUG." FRED ASTAIRE AND GINGER ROGERS

– BELOW –

"CUT WITH QUICK EVEN STROKES." JULIA CHILD

U OF TEXAS – TOWNES LAW

Dogma is man's best friend.

– below –

He had a long-dogma look.

– below –

Fighting like catsmas and dogmas.

– below –

Waiting for Godogma.

– below –

"I wouldn't send a knight out on a dogma like this." (King of France, refusing to participate in the 5th Crusade on religious grounds.)

– below –

Hounded by unjust dogmas.

– below –

The Central Dogma.

– below –

Every dogma has its day.

– below –

Beat a dogma with a stigma.

– below –

Look Ma! No dog!

– below –

Dogmas—a religious holiday for canines.

– below –

Deputy Dogma.

– below –

Inflatible dogmas.

– below –

Raining catherters and dogmas.

– below –

IN-A-GA-DOGMA-VI-DA

– below –

Dogmas at play.

– below –

Hot dogma!

– below –

Order now! Not available in any store! It's Ronco Dogmatic!

– below –

A boy and his dogma.

– below –

Dogma day afternoon.

– below –

It's a dogma eat dogma world.

– below –

Straw dogmas.

U of Texas – Townes Law

A snoid is a small enzyme known for its many variations.

RICE – RAYZOR HALL

Southwest Conference graffitiists often treat their art quite seriously. Here, for example, they help dispense newly discovered scientific knowledge on the campus of Rice University.

Sigmund Freud snoid

Myopoid Snoid

Mummoid Snoid

Void Snoid

Ellipsoid Snoid

Boid Toid Snoid

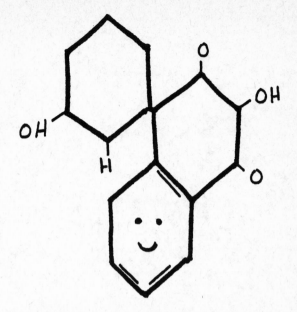

AlKaloid Snoid

Nukoid Snoid

When puns are outlawed, only outlaws will have puns.

From "Crime and Punishment"

We know where he's punning from!

Arkansas – Vol Walker Hall

Then again, sometimes the Southwest graffitiists aren't all that serious.

RADIATION AREA: PRE-FADED GENES ONLY.

HOUSTON – SCIENCE BUILDING

RADIATION IS A BLAST!

TEXAS A&M – TEAGUE RESEARCH CENTER

Microwaves frizz your heir.

Houston – Science Building

I AM A MARXIST WITH GROUCHO TENDENCIES.

U OF TEXAS –
BUSINESS/ECONOMICS

Cellos are basse

Houston – Fine Arts

BE TRUE TO YOUR TEETH AND THEY WILL NEVER BE
FALSE TO YOU.

TEXAS A&M – SCOATES HALL

WHAT DO YOU DO WITH PARASITES?

– BELOW –

SEND THEM BACK TO PARAS.

HOUSTON – ENGINEERING
BUILDING

If he is suffering from phlebitis, why isn't he wearing a phle
collar?

U of Texas – Taylor Hall

MICROBIOLOGY LAB: STAPH ONLY.

HOUSTON – SCIENCE BUILDING

134

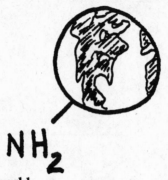

It's amino world.

Texas A&M – Teague Research Center

GONE CHOPIN—BE BACH IN A MINUTE.

– BELOW –

I'M AFRAID SOME JUNG KID WROTE THIS.
HOUSTON – FINE ARTS

I THINK I ZEOLITE AT THE END OF THE TUNNEL.
RICE – GEOLOGY

Infinity is far out!

Texas A&M – Teague Research Center

CUT OUT THIS SCHIST.

RICE – GEOLOGY

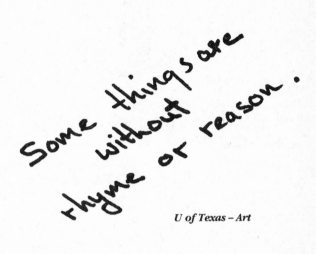

Some things are without rhyme or reason.

U of Texas – Art

All of these limericks rhyme, of course. Their reason is another matter.

THEY SAY THAT THE LADIES IN FRANCE
WEAR LEATHER LINED LACE UNDERPANTS.
WHEN ASKED HOW THEY'RE DOING,
SAY, "I'D RATHER BE SCREWING
THAN TO EAT, OR TO SLEEP, OR TO DANCE."

RICE – ABERCROMBIE LAB

THERE ONCE WAS A PIRATE NAMED GATES
WHO THOUGHT HE COULD RHUMBA ON SKATES.
HE FELL ON HIS CUTLASS
AND NOW IS QUITE NUTLESS,
AND ALSO QUITE USELESS ON DATES.

RICE – ABERCROMBIE LAB

There once was an Aggie named Clyde
who fell in an outhouse and died.
Along came his brother
who fell in another,
and now they're in turd side by side.

U of Texas – Townes Law

THERE WAS A YOUNG STUDENT IN TURMOIL
OVER RELATIONS WITH PROFS BEING FORMAL
SO SHE WENT ON THE MAKE
TILL THE STRAIN GOT TOO GREAT
'CAUSE THE PROFS STRESSED HER FAULTS
WHICH SHE THOUGHT NORMAL.

RICE – GEOLOGY

There once was a man from Kazoo
who really had nothing to do.
So, taking a carrot,
he buggered his parrot,
and sent the results to the zoo.

U of Texas – Moore Hall

THERE WAS A YOUNG MAN FROM LIVERPOOL
WHO HAD A RED RING 'ROUND HIS TOOL.
HE WENT TO THE CLINIC
TO SEE THE DOCTOR, A CYNIC,
WHO SAID, "WASH IT, IT'S LIPSTICK, YOU FOOL."

ARKANSAS – SCIENCE

OLD MOTHER HUBBARD
WENT TO HER CUPBOARD
TO GET HER POOR DOG A BONE.
BUT WHEN SHE BENT OVER
ROVER TOOK OVER
AND GAVE HER A BONE OF HIS OWN.

RICE – ANDERSON BIO LABS

There once was a plumber named Lee
who was plumbing his wife by the sea.
She said, "Stop your plumbing,
there's somebody coming."
"I know," said the plumber, "It's me."

Texas Tech – Holden Hall

THERE WAS A PRIEST FROM NEW DELHI NAMED
KELLY
WHO HAD THE LORD'S PRAYER TATOOED ON HIS
BELLY.
BY THE TIME THAT THE BRAHMIN
HAD READ TO THE "AMEN"
HE HAD BLOWN BOTH SALVATION AND KELLY.

HOUSTON – LIBRARY

No comment!

Rice – Anderson Bio Lab

QUOTE OF THE CENTURY: "DUE TO TECHNICAL DIFFICULTIES."

HOUSTON – FLEMING BUILDING

THE GHOST OF TOMORROW HAS TAKEN MY SOUL.

U OF TEXAS – MOORE HALL

What ever happened to the psychedelic 60's?

Texas Tech – Science

THE SUN IS THE SAME IN A RELATIVE WAY, BUT YOU'RE OLDER.

TEXAS A&M – ZACHARY
ENGINEERING CENTER

186,000 miles per second—it's not just a good idea, it's the law.

– below –

It's a law we can live with.

U of Texas – Townes Law

AND GOD SAID "$e^x c^x = e^x + c$ *AND* THEN *THERE WAS LIGHT.*

U OF TEXAS – WOOLRICH HALL

IGNORE ALL ALIEN ORDERS.

U OF TEXAS – WINSHIP DRAMA BUILDING

Flash Bazbo, Space Explorer, is being tortured on the 4th floor by the Atomic Mind Gobblers from Planet X. Somebody help, please!

– below –

I don't want to get involved. Sorry.

U of Texas – Woolrich Hall

WHO IS SLIM WHITMAN?

ARKANSAS – COMMUNICATIONS

Who was John Galt?

U of Texas – Moore Hall

KENNY THE MONSTER WAS HERE.

RICE – BIOLOGY

Kilroy was here!

So was his mother.

BAYLOR – RICHARDSON SCIENCE

Good Morning, Mr. Phelps.

SMU – Fincher Building

СКОРО БУДЕТ РЕВОЛЦЦИЯ !

> TEXAS A&M – TEAGUE
> RESEARCH CENTER

E Pluribus Fecundum.

> *U of Texas – Moore Hall*

IHR WERDET DIE WAHRHEIT ERKENNEN, UND DIE WAHRHEIT EUCH VOGEL FREI MACHEN.

> *U OF TEXAS – MOORE HALL*

ICH BIN DER CHROME DINETTE.

> *U OF TEXAS – MOORE HALL*

Hurray for oranges!
Go bananas!

> *Texas Tech – Library*

HAVE YOU EVER HAD A HOT DOG THAT WASN'T CIRCUMCIZED?

> *TEXAS A&M – ENGINEERING
> BUILDING*

Alligators don't wear shoes.

U of Texas – Moore Hall

WHATEVER HAPPENED TO ALLIGATOR BAGS?

– BELOW –

WHAT EVER HAPPENED TO $10 BAGS?

ARKANSAS – SCIENCE BUILDING

ROSES ARE RED
VIOLETS ARE BLUE,
SOME POEMS RHYME,
BUT THIS ONE DOESN'T.

U OF TEXAS – UNDERGRADUATE
LIBRARY

The world today is such a wicked place.

U of Texas – Moore Hall

THERE IS NO PLACE.

TEXAS TECH – LIBRARY

Watch out for the anal nitrate.

Texas Tech – Chemistry

STOP DNA RECOMBINATION EXPERIMENTS:
SOCIETY FOR THE PREVENTION OF CRUELTY TO E COLI.

HOUSTON – SCIENCE BUILDING

*TEXAS A&M – BIOLOGICAL
SCIENCES*

Why are there no blue M&M's?

Texas A&M – Engineering Building

TAPE A TOASTER TO YOUR EYELASH.

*U OF TEXAS – WINSHIP DRAMA
BUILDING*

We take a simple pleasure from the rain.

Arkansas – Communications

*AND THEN INDIA THRUST UP INTO ASIA IN ONE SPASM
OF OROGENOUS ECSTASY.*

U OF TEXAS – GEOLOGY

BEWARE THE STERILIZERS!

U OF TEXAS – MOORE HALL

The mouse is loose!

Texas Tech – English

THE MOUSE POLICE NEVER SLEEP!

TEXAS CHRISTIAN – WINTON
SCOTT HALL

Grammaticalophobe!

Texas A&M – Harrington Tower

YOU CAN LEAD A GUITAR TO WATER, BUT YOU CAN'T TUNE A FISH.

U OF TEXAS – GEOLOGY

HURRAY FOR CHRISTMAS!

TEXAS TECH – CHEMISTRY

Is there anyone out there?

Baylor – Marrs McLean Science

BASEBALL HAS BEEN GOOD TO ME.

ARKANSAS – WATERMAN HALL

Free the people from themselves.

Texas A&M – Biological Sciences

THE PEOPLE MUST BE KEPT SIMPLE LIKE THE UNCARVED BLOCK.

U OF TEXAS – GOLDSMITH HALL

HOLD YOUR BREATH AND TURN BLUE, AMERICA.

U OF TEXAS – MOORE HALL

Reunite Gwondonaland!

– below –

Reunite white on ice.

U of Texas – Townes Law

SAVE ME FROM MY MADNESS.

ARKANSAS – WATERMAN HALL

Dandruff is the first sign of madness.

Texas A&M – Teague Research
Center

THE FORCE BE WITH YOU.

RICE – ANDERSON BIOLOGY LAB

B-tha
B-tha
B-tha
B-that's all folks!

—Porky Pig
U of Texas – Geology

You can make it with a little help from your friends.

After having read the previous chapters, a number of you have undoubtedly decided to move to the Southwest, or, more particularly, to attend one of the universities of the Southwest Conference. In that case, we want to suggest several things that you should plan to take with you.

If you are going to Texas Christian University or Southern Methodist University, you should take along a smile. Wear it often; everyone else will be wearing his.

If you are modest and headed for Southern Methodist, you may want to take along a portable stall divider. An economy-minded architect furnished a number of buildings at SMU with stall dividers that are only shoulder high—sitting.

Those going to Arkansas should bring a football, a basketball, and some hill-climbing shoes. This is the hilliest campus in the Southwest Conference.

At Rice you will want a good sense of humor, a high IQ, an alternate food supply, and a good hedge trimmer, should you want to make a quick exit.

If you are going to Houston, you should have a map of any streets other than the freeways and some "uptown" things—this is a big-city school.

Anyone going to Texas A&M would be well advised to pick up an Army manual and a medium-sized carton of Gung-Ho.

Texas Tech should be arrived at with a Western outlook, because that is where you are, in the West.

Ladies going to Baylor should not be without nylons, high heels, and hair curlers.

If you choose the University of Texas to attend, you will want some good walking shoes, as this is the largest campus in the Southwest Conference. Also you might consider investing in a songbook—the carillon tower seems to play just about any song with which you would care to sing along.

Finally, any student in any school in the Southwest Conference other than Texas A&M should know at least ten Aggie jokes. This should not be difficult, as there are hundreds available, and everyone knows some to pass on to you.

KNOCK YOUR SOCKS OFF!!!

See what other campuses are up to from the *inside*!!

GRAFFITI IN THE IVY LEAGUE
(and thereabouts)

Looking for the Northeast universities' secrets of success, our researchers probed past the ivy-covered halls to the scrawl-covered walls. They selected from the genius graffiti the significant, the symbolic, the succinct and the smutty. Now, it's up to you to crack the codes or crack up reading GRAFFITI IN THE IVY LEAGUE (and thereabouts).

available in quality paperback
V37003-7 (U.S.A.)
V37082-7 (Canada)

GRAFFITI IN THE PAC TEN

Out along the Pacific where students at the PAC Ten universities live under the volcano, being faithful to a Fault, or climbing every mountain because it's there—our researchers went fearlessly to search the stalls where the young bare their souls (and other things) and find the PAC-facts. Here it is: the best of the West, the greatest graffiti east of Tahiti—gathered with care before the whole dad-blamed coast falls into the sea.

A quality paperback original
V37002-9 (U.S.A.)
V37083-5 (Canada)

GRAFFITI IN THE BIG TEN

To gather these immortal scrawlings, our researchers penetrated to the ultimate inner sancta—the toilet stalls—plumbing the very depths of the thinking of students at the universities of the Upper Midwest. Here is the collection—profane, profound and profuse. And FUNNY!!

A Warner quality paperback
V37001-0 (U.S.A.)
V37081-9 (Canada)

Each book priced at $4.50 (U.S.A.) and $4.95 in Canada.

SHARE YOUR FAVORITE GRAFFITI WITH US.

No purchase is necessary to qualify. Simply send in your favorite pieces of graffiti on a 3 x 5 index card along with the source of your pieces (for example, campus building and name of school). If they are used in forthcoming sequels of our graffiti books, you will be notified and sent a free copy of our next great book.

Send to:
Reader's Favorite Graffiti
Brown House Galleries
P.O. Box 4243
Madison, WI 53711

Submission of favorite graffiti by readers constitutes your permission for accepted graffiti to be published in any sequels.

—MARINA N. HAAN
—RICHARD B. HAMMERSTROM